P9-CQW-519

Fun In Bed

EDITED BY

Alice Scully

SIMON AND SCHUSTER   *New York*

ACKNOWLEDGMENTS

The author wishes to express appreciation and thanks to the following for their permission to quote from the sources mentioned:

Richard Armour and McGraw-Hill Book Company: *The Medical Muse,* by Richard Armour, copyright © 1963 by Richard Armour.

John Armstrong: *There Was a Young Lady Named Alice,* by John Armstrong, copyright © 1963 by John Armstrong, published by Dell Publishing Co., Inc.

Associated Press: "Strange New World," copyright © 1966 by the Associated Press.

Bernard Geis Associates: *A Child's Garden of Misinformation,* harvested by Art Linkletter, copyright © 1965 by Bernard Geis Associates.

Nelson Buhler, Trustee of Trust created by Laura Baker Cobb, widow of Irvin S. Cobb: *A Laugh a Day Keeps the Doctor Away,* by Irvin S. Cobb, copyright renewed 1950 by Laura Baker Cobb.

Bennett Cerf: *Laughter Incorporated,* by Bennett Cerf, copyright 1950 by Bennett Cerf, published by Doubleday & Company, Inc.

Stan Delaplane: *Postcard from San Francisco,* by Stan Delaplane, copyright 1966 by San Francisco Chronicle Features, originally published in the San Francisco *Chronicle.*

Frederick Fell, Inc.: *For Doctors Only,* by Dr. Francis Leo Golden, copyright 1948 by Frederick Fell, Inc.

Harry Golden: "Going to the Doctor," copyright © 1966 by Harry Golden, published by World Publishing Co.

Leonard L. Levinson: *Webster's Unafraid Dictionary,* by Leonard Louis Levinson, copyright © 1967 by Leonard L. Levinson, published by Collier Books, The Macmillan Company.

Juliet Lowell and M. S. Mill Company, Inc., an affiliate of William Morrow and Company, Inc.: *Dear Doctor,* by Juliet Lowell, copyright © 1955 by Juliet Lowell.

McIntosh & Otis, Inc.: *Letters to Alicia,* by John Steinbeck, copyright © 1966 by John Steinbeck.

The Editor of *Mind* and Sidney Cohen, M.D.: "Fantasy

SBN 671-20398-3
LIBRARY OF CONGRESS CATALOG CARD NUMBER: 72-92196
DESIGNED BY IRVING PERKINS
MANUFACTURED IN THE UNITED STATES OF AMERICA
PRINTED BY DEVEN LITHOGRAPHERS, INC.
BOUND BY SLOVES MECHANICAL BINDING CO., INC.

I would like to express my gratitude for much help and wonderful encouragement to M. Lincoln Schuster, Silas F. Seadler, Lorna D. Smith, Rose and Bob Lane, Mary Stone, Dr. Charles McCammon, Marge Maniaci, Janice Madsen, Anne Gougler, Helen Colton, Leonard L. Levinson, Herkie Styles, Pat and Harry Wilson, Cornelia Sussman, Bea and Lee Mishkin and Charlotte Seitlin.

ALICE SCULLY

To

FRANK

Contents

INTRODUCTION   11

ACT I   *Open Here*   13

ACT II   *Game Preserve*   21

ACT III   *Department of Labor*   39

ACT IV   *It's All in Your Mind*   47

ACT V   *Horizontal Blues*   59

ACT VI   *Exit Smiling*   67

ANSWERS   75

Introduction

Many years have passed since the original *Fun in Bed* books, edited by that indomitable invalid Frank Scully, first appeared.

Frank Scully, newspaperman and author, died in 1964. He had been an invalid since his teens, but that did not seem to interfere with his education, jobs or life in general. He refused to let his mind "be put in a splint." He developed his sense of humor to the point where he could find a laugh in almost everything. His record of hospitalizations and operations was so long that it would only drag you down if I were to give you the details.

Once while recovering from surgery for an aorta transplant—they had also relieved him of his appendix and gall bladder at the same time—he was flattened out. He lay there on his hospital bed, his face practically contorted with deep thoughts. I asked him what he was thinking. He said he was trying to work up a gag for the doctor because he had made up his mind to give the doctor a laugh each time he came to visit. It used to take him all day at first, but, with that attitude, how can you lose?

Back in the '30s, before TV, when people were well and wanted to be entertained they went to a show. Frank felt that when they were sick the show should come to them. So he compiled and wrote the first of his six *Fun in Bed* books.

Although treatments have changed since those days, we still come down with the same old diseases. What was considered dangerous back in the b.a.b. (before antibiotics) era can now be thrown off with the help of pills or injections. Everything, that is, except the common cold. Nevertheless, we still have to go to hospitals. Humor, of course, is based on someone else's mishap or loss of dignity. Where but in a hospital is all dignity and modesty stripped from us? While waiting for something to happen, or recovering from The Happening, we still get worried or bored and need something to cheer us up.

Here, then, is a new *Fun in Bed*, designed so that it can be put aside during those continual interruptions for temperatures and tests and picked up again without losing the thread. I hope it will help you to enjoy a little humor about your own situation as well as that of those around you. Some of the jokes and stories are new, others are old, but there is comfort in old stories as well as old friends.

So let's get on with the show.

ALICE SCULLY

11

ACT I *Open Here*

NOTED IN AN OLD ENGLISH CATHEDRAL

Give me a sense of humor, Lord,
Give me grace to see a joke,
To get some happiness from Life
And pass it on to other folk.

❦

GOOD ADVICE

Thirty years ago Dr. James J. Walsh, then medical director of the Fordham School of Sociology, prescribed frequent laughter as an antidote for many bodily disorders. "Technically, laughter is the excursion of the diaphragm, which massages organs in the chest and abdomen, but other than that, it is nature's tonic," he said, "fully as important as any exercise for an individual's health."

Then we found that after abdominal surgery laughing might be extremely painful, so the good

Dr. Arthur Seligman suggested a procedure for preventing laughter. "The trick is to open your mouth as wide as possible and keep it set for a while . . . Then you're laughproof."

Still, that doesn't prevent you from feeling happy when you hear a funny story.

❦

RIGHT NUMBER

"Dr. Smith's office," my receptionist said in answering the telephone.

There was no reply for a moment, then a tremulous female voice asked, "Is this really Dr. Smith's office?"

"Yes, it is," said the receptionist. "Did you wish to speak to Dr. Smith?"

There was an embarrassed silence. Then the female voice said softly, "I guess not. I just found this phone number in the pocket of my husband's coat."   R. D.

"Now, all together—say 'Hmmmmmmmmmm.'"

Cartoon by JACK MARKOW, © 1965 by Saturday Review, Inc.

BY APPOINTMENT ONLY

Waiting at the doctor's,
Waiting in the cab,
Waiting in the office,
Waiting in the lab.

Waiting for the X ray
Waiting for the knife,
Waiting for the daylight,
Waiting half your life.

Everybody's lagging,
Everything is late;
Pain alone is punctual;
Pain can never wait.

FRANK SCULLY

GOING TO THE DOCTOR

Zeus and his wife, Hera, the gods who ruled mythical Mount Olympus, had an argument one afternoon about who enjoyed love more: men or women.

Unable to come to an amicable decision, they dispatched the prophet Teiresias to earth, where he put in seven years as a man and seven years as a woman. When Teiresias reported back he said, "Women." Hera was so mad at losing an argument she blinded him.

I'd like to find a modern Teiresias and ask him about who enjoys going to the doctor more: men or women.

I think it would be unfair to batter poor Teiresias up with broken legs and earaches and rheumy eyes. No. I wouldn't give him any disease or injuries, just normal health and chart how many times he went to the doctor as the man and how many times as the woman.

There are several reasons why men go to the doctor. The chief of these often is that they don't feel well. They are heir to as many ills and complaints as anyone.

A second reason men go to the doctor is that their wives make them go. By their lights. I suppose, there's much to be said for a visit to the doctor when no one is sick. I have always felt, however, that's looking for trouble.

The ladies hie themselves to the doctor on every conceivable occasion. Perhaps they are closer to the earth than men, but women can cherish ill health sometimes like a mother cherishes a child.

A gynecologist has hardly any leisure, but if it weren't for tough drill sergeants, Army doctors would go crackers from boredom on a stateside base. Recruits have to be marched over for their shots and checkups. Very possibly women get in the habit of going to the doctor because they bear children. Certainly they have more time for it than men.

I suppose if I had nothing to do I would either go to the doctor or help out with the PTA or maybe join a Sodality or at least the League of Women Voters so I could discuss my medical history in concert with others.

Teiresias would tell them, "Women like going to the doctor better than men. But," he would add, "they live longer down there so there must be something to it."

HARRY GOLDEN

A new doctor giving an old lady a complete physical, more complete than she had ever had, was asked afterwards, "Young man, does your mother know how you are making a living?"

QUICK SERVICE

Patients are impatient folk
Who will not wait to hear a joke
Or even pass the time of day,
But want their health back, right away.

They hate to sit there one full minute,
Mouth shut (thermometer jammed in it).
They can't bear waiting, not a bit,
For wounds to heal and bones to knit.

They want to be all well at once.
If you can't do it, you're a dunce.
And though they summon a physician,
They really need a good magician.

RICHARD ARMOUR

Mrs. Brown was complaining to her doctor that his bill was unreasonably high. "Don't forget," he reminded her, "that I made eleven visits to your home while your son had the measles."

"And don't you forget," she countered, "that he infected the whole school."

"It says he has the sniffles."

Cartoon by SLIM, © 1965 by *Modern Medicine.*

"The real enigma, of course, is that she seems to have what she says she has."

Cartoon by BOB JOHNSON, © 1966 by *Modern Medicine*.

"How did she ever come down with infectious mononucleosis?"

Cartoon by JOHN MORRIS, © 1966 by *Modern Medicine*.

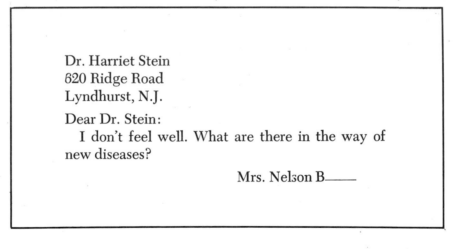

Dr. Harriet Stein
620 Ridge Road
Lyndhurst, N.J.

Dear Dr. Stein:

I don't feel well. What are there in the way of new diseases?

Mrs. Nelson B——

Cartoon by M. LEUNG, © 1967 by Parade Publications, Inc.

Nellie Nifty, R.N.

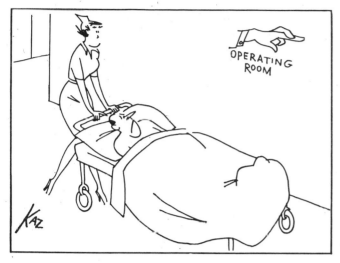

Cartoon by KAZ, © 1966 by *Modern Medicine*.

BEFORE THE OPERATION

One of the best ways to prepare for an operation is to *think* of it in the past.

As you pack your bag for the hospital, say, "By this time tomorrow night I'll be rid of this murderous pain."

When you reach your bed and they give you what the nurses so irreverently call "the three H's" (high, hot and a hell-of-a-lot), you say, "by next week that will be something to laugh about."

In the morning when they prepare you for the ride on an empty stomach, say, "When they bathe me tomorrow, it will be for breakfast."

As they wheel you toward the ether emporium, say, "At this hour tomorrow they will have given me orders to get up and walk around."

As they strap you to the operating table, say gaggingly, "Well, it's never too late to mend, is it?"

As they place the anesthetic mask over you . . .
Say your prayers!

A LITTLE LEARNING

Patients once let surgeons cut
Without an if or and or but.
They rarely raised demanding questions
And never offered up suggestions.

Patients once, not long ago,
Believed the doctor ought to know,
Submitted with the best of will,
And trusted in his practiced skill.

But patients now, and patients' wives,
Are sharper than a surgeon's knives,
And argue over each incision. . . .
They've seen it all on television.

RICHARD ARMOUR

"Now, don't go away. I'll be back after lunch."
Cartoon by DAVID HARBAUGH, © 1967 by *Modern Medicine*.

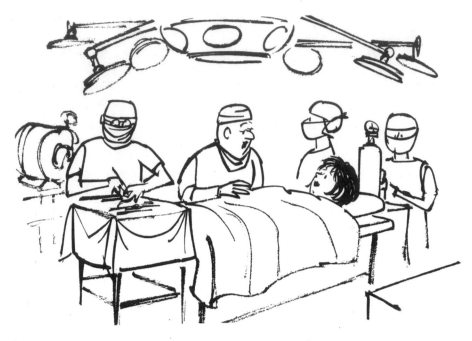

"I don't have a brochure of scars to show you.
You'll just have to take pot luck."

Cartoon by AL KAUFMAN, © 1966 by The American Medical Association.

"Okay, let's do it. I'll try anything once."

Cartoon by SLIM, © 1966 by *Modern Medicine*.

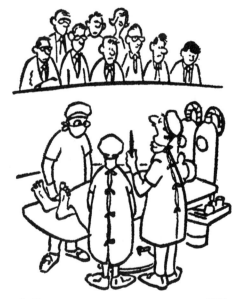

"Always cut away *from yourself!"*

Cartoon by E. N., © 1968 by Gates Features, Inc.

Dr. Snaps was a kibitzer from way back. His office was above the drugstore. In back of the store was a room where a group gathered to play all kinds of poker and other games. One day while checking one of his patients he put a thermometer in his mouth, warning him to keep it in till he came back. He then went down to the drugstore to pick up some potion. While there, he peeked in at the game in the back room and began kibitzing, completely forgetting his patient. Two hours later he retired to his office. Very embarrassed, he took the thermometer out, looked at it, put it back and said, "Just a few minutes more."

A maiden at college, Miss Breeze,
Weighed down by B.A.'s and Ph.D.'s.
   Collapsed from the strain.
   Said her doctor, "It's plain
You are killing yourself—by degrees!"

LEONARD LOUIS LEVINSON

OPERATING THEATER

This is the hour that invalids dread,
The time when nurses smile and touch your head,
And shoot your arm with sedifying drugs,
Which calm you like lead pipes of thugs.
This is the moment for taking you from bed,
To roll you to the place where blood is shed,
Where basins take the place of rugs,
And painful organs find themselves in jugs.

This is the time for praying that the hand
Which guides the surgeon's knife in search of pain
May do exactly as the doctors planned
When diagnosing you—their No Man's Land.
The time when all is lost and you are slain,
Or all is won and you're yourself again.

FRANK SCULLY

Surgeons of ancient Egypt put their patients to sleep by hitting them on the head.

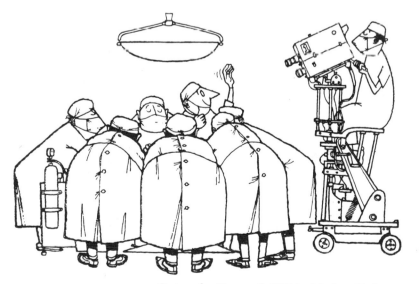

Cartoon by MOSER, © 1965 by *Modern Medicine*.

"I had to shave myself this morning!"

Cartoon by ED REED, © by Des Moines Register & Tribune Syndicate.

ACT II *Game Preserve*

GAME PRESERVE

Whether you're marooned in a hospital, a sanatorium, or picking crumbs from a counterpane at home, the first days of convalescence seem to take *years* to pass.

Just horsing around waiting to get well is the ultimate irritant. Often you feel so crabby that if you could get out of bed you'd probably find yourself walking backwards.

To escape such an intolerable situation you can either list all the pains that have cropped up since the doctor's last visit (pains which certainly will leave you like rats deserting a sinking ship when he *does* finally come) or you can grit your teeth, bite your pencil, and dig into the games and gags which follow.

Of the two, it may be that you prefer neither. In that case throw the book through a window and see what happens.

The funny part of it is that the games are not like doctor's promises; these actually come off. Each problem has its solution. But don't let success go to your head.

If you begin dozing before you finish one of the games, you've hit on the cure of all cures. In that case, sleep till they wake you up with the dinner tray, and then try some more games till you hit the land of nod again. And don't mind mistakes. That's what erasers are for.

DO YOU WANT TO MAKE SOMETHING OUT OF IT?

Or, if you put an "O" on "Understo,"
you'll ruin my "Thunderstorm"

I'm probably not the oldest word-game player in the country, and I know I'm not the ablest, but my friends will all testify that I'm the doggedest. (We'll come back to the word "doggedest" later on.) I sometimes keep on playing the game, all by myself, after it is over and I have gone to bed. On a recent night, tossing and spelling, I spent two hours hunting for another word besides "phlox" that has "hlo" in it. I finally found seven: "matchlock," "decathlon," "pentathlon," "hydrochloric," "chlorine," "chloroform," and "monthlong." There are more than a dozen others, beginning with "phlo," but I had to look them up in the dictionary the next morning, and that doesn't count.

By "the game," I mean Superghosts, as some of us call it, a difficult variation of the familiar parlor game known as Ghosts. In Ghosts, as everybody knows, one of a group of sedentary players starts with a letter, and the spelling proceeds clockwise around the group until a player spells a word of more than three letters, thus becoming "a third of a ghost," or two-thirds, or a whole ghost. The game goes on until everyone but the winner has been eliminated. Superghosts differs from the old game in one small, tricky, and often exacerbating respect: The rules allow a player to *prefix* a letter to the word in progress, thus increasing the flexibility of the indoor sport. If "busines" comes to a player, he does not have to add the final "s"; he can put an "n" in front, and the player who has to add the "e" to "unbusinesslik" becomes part of a ghost. In a recent game in my league, a devious gentleman boldly stuck an "n" in front of "sobsiste," stoutly maintaining the validity of "unsobsisterlike," but he was shouted down. There is a lot of shouting in the game, especially when it is played late at night.

Starting words in the middle and spelling them in both directions lifts the pallid pastime of Ghosts out of the realm of children's parties and ladies' sewing circles and makes it a game to test the mettle of the mature adult mind. As long ago as 1930, aficionados began to appear in New York parlors, and then the game waned, to be revived, in my circle, last year. The Superghost aficionado is a moody fellow, given to spelling to himself at table, not listening to his wife, and staring dully at his frightened children, wondering why he didn't detect, in yesterday's game, that "cklu" is the guts of "lacklustre," and priding himself on having stumped everybody with "nehe," the middle of "swineherd." In this last case, "bonehead" would have done, since we allow slang if it is in the dictionary, but "Stonehenge" is out, because we don't allow proper nouns. All compound and hyphenated words are privileged, even "jack-o'-lantern" and "love-in-a-mist," but the speller must indicate where a hyphen occurs.

Many people, who don't like word games and just want to sit around and drink and talk, hate Superghosts and wish it were in hell with Knock, Knock, Who's There? The game is also tough on bad spellers, poor visualizers, mediocre concentrators, ladies and gentlemen of small vocabulary, and those who are, to use a word presently popular with the younger drinking set, clobbered. I remember the night a bad speller, female, put an "m" on "ale," thinking, as she later confessed, that "salamander" is spelled with two "e"s. The next player could have gone to "alemb"—the word "alembic" turns up a lot—but he made it "alema" and was promptly challenged. (You can challenge a player if you think he is bluffing.) What the challenged player had in mind was "stalemate." The man who had challenged him got sore, because he hadn't thought of "stalemate," and went home. More than one game has ended in hard feelings, but I have never seen players come to blows, or friendships actually broken.

I said we would get back to "doggedest," and here we are. This word, if it is a word, caused a lot of trouble during one game, when a lady found "ogged" in her lap, refused to be bogged, dogged, fogged, jogged, or logged, and added an "e." She was challenged and lost, since Webster's unabridged dictionary is accepted as the final judge and authority, and while it gives "doggedly" and "doggedness," it doesn't give "doggedest." She could also have got out of "ogged" with an "r" in front, for "frogged" is a good word, and also what might be called a lady's word, but she stuck doggedly to "doggedest." Then there was the evening a dangerous and exasperating player named Bert Mitchell challenged somebody's "dogger." The challenged man had "doggerel" in mind, of course, but Mitchell said, in his irritating voice, "You have spelled a word. 'Dogger' is a word," and he flipped through the unabridged dictionary, which he reads for pleasure and always has on his lap during a game. "Dogger" is indeed a word, and quite a word. Look it up yourself.

When I looked up "dogger" the other day, I decided to have a look at "dog," a word practically nobody ever looks up, because everybody is smugly confident that he knows what a dog is. Here for your amazement, are some dogs other than the carnivorous mammal:

The hammer in a gunlock. Any of various devices, usually of simple design, for holding, gripping, or fastening something; as: **a** Any of various devices consisting essentially of a spike, rod, or bar of metal, as of iron, with a ring, hook, claw, lug, or the like, at the end, used for gripping, clutching, or holding something, as by driving or embedding it in the object, hooking it to the object, etc. See RAFT DOG, TOE DOG. **b** Specif., either of the hooks or claws of a pair of sling dogs. See CRAMPON. **c** An iron for holding wood in a fireplace; a firedog; an andiron. **d** In a lathe, a clamp for gripping the piece of work and for communicating motion to it from the faceplate. A *clamp dog* consists of two parts drawn together by screws. A *bent-tail dog* has an L-shaped projection that enters a slot in the faceplate for communicating motion. A *straight-tail dog* has a projecting part that engages with a stud fastened to or forming part of the faceplate. A *safety dog* is one equipped with safety setscrews. **e** Any of the jaws in a lathe chuck. **f** A pair of nippers or forceps. **g** A wheeled gripping device for drawing the fillet from which coin blanks are stamped through the opening at the head of the drawbench. **h** Any of a set of adjusting screws for the bed tool of a punching machine. **i** A grapple for clutching and raising a pile-driver monkey or a well-boring tool. **j** A stop or detent; a click or ratchet. **k** A drag for the wheel of a vehicle. **l** A steel block attached to a locking bar or tappet of an interlocking machine by which locking between bars is accomplished. **m** A short, heavy, sharp-pointed, steel hook with a ring at one end. **n** A steel toothlike projection on a log carriage or on the endless chain that conveys logs into the sawmill.

And now, unless you have had enough, we will get back to Superghosts, through the clanging and clatter of all those dogs. The game has a major handicap, or perhaps I should call it blockage. A player rarely gets the chance to stick the others with a truly tough word, because someone is pretty sure to simplify the word under construction.

Mitchell tells me that he always hopes he can get around to "ug-ug" or "ach-ach" on his way to "plug-ugly" and "stomach-ache." These words are hyphenated in my Webster's, for the old boy was a great hyphenator. (I like his definition of "plug-ugly": "A kind of city rowdy, ruffian, or disorderly tough;—a term said to have been originated by a gang of such in Baltimore.") In the case of "ug," the simplifiers usually go to "bug," trying to catch someone with "buggies," or they add an "l" and the word ends in "ugliness." And "ach" often turns into "machinery," although it could go in half a dozen directions. Since the simplifiers dull the game by getting into easy words, the experts are fond of a variant that goes like this: Mitchell, for example, will call up a friend and say, "Get out of 'ightf' twenty ways." Well, I tossed in bed one night and got ten: "rightful," "frightful," "delightful," "nightfall," "lightfoot," "straightforward," "eightfold," "light-fingered," "tight-fisted," and "tight-fitting." The next day, I thought of "lightface," "right-footed," and "night-flowering," and came to a stop. "Right fielder" is neither compounded nor hyphenated by Webster, and I began to wonder about Mitchell's twenty "ightf"'s. I finally figured it out. The old devil was familiar with ten or more fish and fowl and miscellaneous things that begin with "nightf."

It must have been about 1932 that an old player I know figured that nothing could be got out of "dke" except "handkerchief," and then, in a noisy game one night this year, he passed that combination on to the player at his left. This rascal immediately made it "dkee." He was challenged by the lady on *his* left and triumphantly announced that his word was "groundkeeper." It looked like an ingenious escape from "handkerchief," but old Webster let the fellow down. Webster accepts only "groundman" and "groundsman," thus implying that there is no such word as "groundkeeper."

Mitchel threw "abc" at me one night, and I couldn't get anything out of it and challenged him. "Dabchick," he said patronizingly, and added blandly, "It is the little grebe." Needless to say, it *is* the little grebe.

I went through a hundred permutations in bed

that night without getting anything else out of "abc" except a word I made up, which is "grab-check," one who quickly picks up a tab, a big spender, a generous fellow. I have invented quite a few other words, too, which I modestly bring to the attention of modern lexicographers, if there are any. I think of dictionary-makers as being rigidly conventional gentlemen who are the first to put the new aside. They probably won't even read my list of what I shall call bedwords, but I am going to set it down anyway. A young matron in Bermuda last spring told me to see what I could do with "sgra," and what I did with it occupied a whole weekend. Outside of "disgrace" and "grosgrain," all I could find were "cross-grained" and "misgraff," which means to misgraft (obsolete). I found this last word while looking, in vain, for "misgrade" in the dictionary. Maybe you can think of something else, and I wish you luck. Here, then, in no special order, are my bedwords based on "sgra."

Pussgrapple. A bickering, or minor disturbance; an argument or dispute among effeminate men. Also, less frequently, a physical struggle between, or among, women.

Kissgranny. 1. A man who seeks the company of older women, especially older women with money; a designing fellow, a fortune hunter. 2. An overaffectionate old woman, a hugmoppet, a bunnytalker.

Glassgrabber. 1. A woman who disapproves of, or interferes with, her husband's drinking; a killjoy, a shushlaugh, a douselight. 2. A man who asks for another drink at a friend's house, or goes out and gets one in the kitchen.

Blessgravy. A minister or cleric; the head of a family; one who says grace. Not to be confused with *praisegravy,* one who extols a woman's cooking, especially the cooking of a friend's wife; a gay fellow, a flirt, a seducer. *Colloq.,* a breakvow, a shrugholy.

Cussgravy. A husband who complains of his wife's cooking, more especially a husband who complains of his wife's cooking in the presence of

guests; an ill-tempered fellow, a curmudgeon. Also, sometimes, a peptic-ulcer case.

Messgranter. An untidy housekeeper, a careless housewife. Said of a woman who admits, often proudly, that she has let herself go; a bragdowdy, a frumpess.

Hissgrammar. An illiterate fellow, a user of slovenly rhetoric, a father who disapproves of book-learning. Also, more rarely, one who lisps, a twisttongue.

Chorusgrable. *Orig.* a young actress, overconfident of her ability and her future; a snippet, a flappertigibbet. *Deriv.* Betty Grable, an American movie actress.

Pressgrape. One who presses grapes, a grape presser. Less commonly, a crunchberry.

Pressgrain. 1. A man who tries to make whiskey in his own cellar; hence, a secret drinker, a hide-bottle, a sneakslug. 2. One who presses grain in a grain presser. *Arch.*

Dressgrader. A woman who stares another woman up and down, a starefrock; hence, a rude female, a hobbledehoydon.

Fussgrape. 1. One who diets or toys with his food, a light eater, a person without appetite, a scornmuffin, a shuncabbage. 2. A man, usually American, who boasts of his knowledge of wines, a smug-bottle.

Bassgrave. 1. Cold-eyed, unemotional, stolid, troutsolemn. 2. The grave of a bass. *Obs.*

Lassgraphic. Of, or pertaining to, the vivid description of females; as, the guest was so lassgraphic his host asked him to change the subject or get out. Also said of fathers of daughters, more rarely of mothers.

Blissgray. Aged by marriage. Also, sometimes, discouraged by wedlock, or by the institution of marriage.

Glassgrail. A large nocturnal moth. Not to be confused with smackwindow, the common June bug, or bangsash.

Hossgrace. Innate or native dignity, similar to that of the thoroughbred hoss. *Southern U.S.*

Bussgranite. Literally, a stonekisser; a man who persists in trying to win the favor or attention of cold, indifferent, or capricious women. Not to be confused with *snatchkiss,* a kitchen lover.

Tossgravel. 1. A male human being who tosses gravel, usually at night, at the window of a female human being's bedroom, usually that of a young virgin; hence, a lover, a male sweetheart, and an eloper. 2. One who is suspected by the father of a daughter of planning an elopement with her, a grablass.

If you should ever get into a game of Superghosts with Mitchell, by the way, don't pass "bugl" on to him, hoping to send him into "bugling." He will simply add an "o," making the group "buglo," which is five-sevenths of "bugloss." The word means "hawkseed," and you can see what Mitchell would do if you handed him "awkw," expecting to make him continue the spelling of "awkward." Tough guy, Mitchell. Tough game, Superghosts. You take it from here. I'm tired.

JAMES THURBER

❦

LETTER-LAUGHS

From childhood Silas F. Seadler, a Columbia classmate of Frank's, has been playing with words. He began by gagging his alphabet blocks, and when informed at age six that Grant took Richmond (this was some time after the event), he wanted to know "with how many letters?"

It wasn't until later, while recuperating from a bout with tuberculosis at Asheville, North Carolina, that he took to the Art of Anagraphing; and later he even compiled an *Anagram Book,* which, lamentably, is long out of print.

But the game itself goes on. It has even created Anagram Widows, who take tea and toast to stave off starvation while waiting for husbands who take "nerve" with an "e" to make "veneer."

To the bored-and-bed-bound, the game should be an easy, fun-filled exercise in word-building. You can play alone, or with someone else; even six can play, although alone or with one friend is best for sick people.

Object of the game is to make new words out of old by adding one letter at a time. Start with four words of four letters and build as long as you can.

If playing with blocks or cubes, it's much like dominoes, with letters instead of numbers. You're allowed a minute to construct a new word with your new letter. Failing, your opponent gets his chance. Each tries to "take" the other's words. A classic conquest was Howard Dietz's capture of "pouches" with a "y," making "chop suey," though Dorothy Parker's "inkpot" by adding a "k" to "point" wasn't so bad either.

There's no end of variations and complications to Anagrams, but why bother your head about them until your temperature is 98.6 and your pulse 72 every day.

Here are a few samples of Anagrams. The first one has been done for you. Now get out your pencil and zip through the others. Answers are in the back of the book. Stay away from there until you've either finished in triumph, or you hit a dead end and your eye has lost its *luster*, then add an "s," which gives you the *results* (which are) on page 75.

I

M U S E with R	S E R U M
R O B E with P	_ _ _ _ _
T H A W with R	_ _ _ _ _
R U N S with E	_ _ _ _ _
O A T S with T	_ _ _ _ _
M A N E with E	_ _ _ _ _
R A T E with H	_ _ _ _ _
T H E E with R	_ _ _ _ _

And here are a few teasers from Si Seadler's *Anagram Book* (see page 75 for answers).

First a couple of simple ones:

II

T O R E with V	_ _ _ _ _
I D E A with S	_ _ _ _ _
W O R D with C	_ _ _ _ _
G O R E with U	_ _ _ _ _

D R O V E with U   _ _ _ _ _ _

N E A R with V   _ _ _ _ _

M A S H with E   _ _ _ _ _

B A L E with T   _ _ _ _ _

L O A D with U   _ _ _ _ _

C R A B with E   _ _ _ _ _

See page 75 for answers.

III

L O W E R with T   _ _ _ _ _ _

R A N G E with D   _ _ _ _ _ _

V I A N D with S   _ _ _ _ _ _

I R A T E with G   _ _ _ _ _ _

D R E A M with I   _ _ _ _ _ _

A T L A S with N   _ _ _ _ _ _

A P P L E with A   _ _ _ _ _ _

I N E P T with S   _ _ _ _ _ _

R I S E N with D   _ _ _ _ _ _

T O N I C with S   _ _ _ _ _ _

And here's an Anagram sequence, in which each word leads to the next.

IV

C A R D with E

_ _ _ _ _ with S

_ _ _ _ _ _ with E

_ _ _ _ _ _ _

B E A T with L

_ _ _ _ _ with S

_ _ _ _ _ _ with D

_ _ _ _ _ _ _

G R A N D with E

_ _ _ _ _ _ with E

_ _ _ _ _ _ _ with D

_ _ _ _ _ _ _

P L E A T with S

_ _ _ _ _ _ with R

_ _ _ _ _ _ _ with E

_ _ _ _ _ _ _ _

And here's a Multiple Anagram. It's surprising what one word will yield. See page 75 for answers.

V

B L A R E with W   _ _ _ _ _ _

B L A R E with G   _ _ _ _ _ _

B L A R E with B   _ _ _ _ _ _

B L A R E with I   _ _ _ _ _ _

A M B L E with D   _ _ _ _ _ _

A M B L E with G   _ _ _ _ _ _

A M B L E with D   _ _ _ _ _ _

A M B L E with R   _ _ _ _ _ _

Toughest of all: taking a word with *two letters*. (Adding O and D would make *toward* out of *wart*, wouldn't it?) See page 75 for answers.

VI

W R A I T H with W and D

    _ _ _ _ _ _ _ _

M O T T O with P and S

    _ _ _ _ _ _ _

A L T A R with U and N

    _ _ _ _ _ _ _

A N T I C with R and U

    _ _ _ _ _ _ _

S H A N K with V and I

    _ _ _ _ _ _ _

S E R V E S with E and R

    _ _ _ _ _ _ _ _

T I R I N G with E and U

    _ _ _ _ _ _ _ _

T A N G L E with I and R

——————————

C L U E S with O and G

——————————

C H A R R E D with G and E

——————————

VII

S A M E with U   —————

S A M E with N   —————

S A M E with R   —————

S A M E with R   —————

S A M E with L   —————

S A M E with L   —————

S A M E with S   —————

S A M E with R   —————

S A M E with B   —————

S A M E with D   —————

S A M E with G   —————

S A M E with T   —————

GAMES

Let no one think for a minute that the reservoir of games for insomniacs is going dry. *Saturday Review* readers have been flooding this desk with enough braintwisters to cause an epidemic of hollow, sunken eyes and ashen cheeks.

Actor Chester Morris wrecks many of his sleeping hours by engaging in a game called Non-Nick-names. It's simple enough, if you hate sleep. All you do is wonder about how many famous celebrities would be practically unrecognizable on a hotel register if they signed in with their full names: Daniel Kaye, John Benny, John Paar, Burton Lancaster, Chester Huntley, Harry Crosby, Edward Sullivan, Peter Berra, Anthony Randall, and so on. But, Mr. Morris notes, the same effect holds if the thinking is reversed: Al Lunt, Betty Taylor.

Ralph Cokain, of New York, has his own method of wrecking his rest. He uses a game he calls Cross-Breed, in which you cross a few unlikely categories and come up with something entirely new. Examples: Cross a British nobleman with a suitmaker. Result—Lord & Taylor, Cross the Pentagon with United Parcel Service. Result—General Delivery. Cross a slide fastener with a telegraph operator. Result—Zip code.

In San Francisco, John Coulthard walks the floor at night with a game he calls Limericryptograms. Example:

> Aim aid din Abe you teepee raid
> Haddock cost tomb inn witchy Dis
>   played
>   Al ursine aweigh
>   Two inn, "Hippo ray!"
> Diddle Ottoman scree, "Mitts sew
>   Kay!"

Translation:

> A maid in a beauty parade
> Had a costume in which she
>   displayed
>   Allures in a way
>   To win, "Hip hooray!"
> Did a lot o' men scream, "It's okay!"

In Winnipeg, Canada, Marian Forer stares at the ceiling, wondering how, if lawyers are disbarred, and priests unfrocked, other people in other walks of life might be read out of their callings.

Examples: Electricians get delighted; musicians denoted; cowboys deranged; models deposed; judges distorted. What's more, mediums are dispirited; dressmakers unbiased; Far Eastern diplomats disoriented; office workers defiled.

In Cleveland, Ohio, Marion Stewart systematically upsets her sleeping cart with a game called Unlikely Enterprises. After a long drive along commercial strips, she has come up with such commercial establishments as Hiawatha's Bavarian Hut, Svenson's Hacienda, Luigi's Igloo, McTavish's Villa, and Stumpf's Chateau, not to mention O'Rafferty's Hofbrau, Ginocopoli's Smorgasbord, de Beaupre's Fish & Chips, and Cassidy's Samovar. Going in a bit stronger for contradictions, she has devised such eating spots as Tiny's Imperial Palace and Thruway-Vue Hideaway.

In Boulder, Colorado, Dorothy Beers manages to while away the hours until dawn by trying to find two words or expressions, one containing the word "up" and the other "down." Examples: shut up, pipe down; upbraid, dress down; lay down one's life, give up the ghost; downcast, upset; close down, fold up; turn one's nose up, look down one's nose at. And if all this isn't enough, Mrs. Beers concludes with: "Can you think of any words beside 'raze' and 'raise' that sound the same but have opposite meanings?"

Urbana, Illinois, is the place where Victor Lukas and F. K. Plous, Jr., sit up half the night finding words in which the first half of a noun is a verb, and the second half is that same verb's direct object. Examples: Breakfast, killjoy, passport, turncoat, cutthroat, scofflaw.

"Nowadays," they write, "such terms seem to get turned around, with the object preceding and the verb following, and an 'er' tacked on to the end —such as 'penny-pincher.' And not only did Shakespeare use such terms—but his own surname falls into the same category."

In Cedarhurst, New York, Walter Gelles challenges Morpheus with a game called Bibliography. For a math term paper, he has devised such unlikely books as: *How to Trap a Zoid, From Here to Infinity, Six Ways to Serve Pi, Don't Be a Square,* and *Knowing the Angles.*

In New York City, Jack Cornwall leaves his bedside lamp on to work on a game called Hollywood Columnist. His mythical columns run something like this: "Dinah Shore last week gave a big swim party welcoming Turhan Bey back to Hollywood. Present were Ernie Banks, Larry Rivers, Veronica Lake, Lily Pons, and Geraldine Brooks. It was quite a fling until Gail Storm blew in with Claude Rains, C. P. Snow, and Curt Flood. . . . Robert Trout was out on the town last night at the Cape Cod Room with Saul Bass and Newton Minow. They were accompanied by Peter Finch, Dean Martin, Anthony Quayle, and Walter Pidgeon, all preparing to fly to Miami."

In Great Neck, New York, thirteen-year-old Sandy Landsman is getting circles under his eyes with his game called Cinepuns. He suggests a documentary film about a rough boat ride between Switzerland and Germany called *Days of Rhine and Woeses,* and a new *Irma La Douce* called *A Distant Strumpet.*

In Newfields, New Hampshire, the Reverend and Mrs. E. F. Stoneham stay awake long after the town has gone to sleep with their game, Speaking Zoologically. "The rules are obvious, and can be changed at will," they note. Examples: Pelican-tankerously, giraffe-ably, elephant-tastically, kangaroo-fully.

JOHN G. FULLER

THE SUN, MOON AND PLANETS

HARRY WILSON

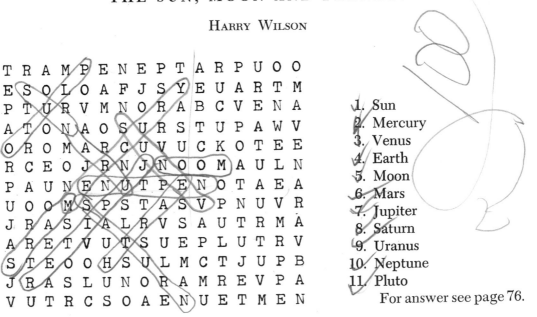

```
T R A M P E N E P T A R P U O O
E S O L O A F J S Y E U A R T M
P T U R V M N O R A B C V E N A
A T O N A O S U R S T U P A W V
O R O M A R C U V U C K O T E E
R C E O J R N J N O O M A U L N
P A U N E N U T P E N O T A E A
U O O M S P S T A S V P N U V R
J R A S I A L R V S A U T R M A
A R E T V U T S U E P L U T R V
S T E O O H S U L M C T J U P B
J R A S L U N O R A M R E V P A
V U T R C S O A E N U E T M E N
```

1. Sun
2. Mercury
3. Venus
4. Earth
5. Moon
6. Mars
7. Jupiter
8. Saturn
9. Uranus
10. Neptune
11. Pluto

For answer see page 76.

ARMCHAIR TOUR OF THE U.S.A.

The names of all fifty states of the U.S.A. can be found among the letters below. The names sometimes read forward, sometimes backward, sometimes up, down, diagonally. Draw a pencil line around the name of a state when you locate the sequence of letters that spells it. For answer see page 76.

```
S T T E S U H C A S S A M T R S M Z A O U R
R E T S K C I K P L B V R S Y A V E M A A W
A N O Z I R A I N I G R I V T S E W I D N Y
A I N R O F I L A C U A Z X Y S R G N I A K
N O T G N I H S A W U N A B S T M E N R I C
S O U T H D A K O T A N E E J J O O E O S U
M A R Y L A N D L M I H N W N O N R S L I T
O P U T A H R S T L N N U E J V T G O F U N
A K A X H O A W O I E Y Z A V E R I T S O E
K R L S B C D R E T F C I J K A R A A X L K
S O A I N A V L Y S N N E P M D S N O P E
A Y S X H C S R N A G I H C I M N A E T U R
R W K E H O W Y O M I N G V S A X Y S Y A H
B E A T C E M F I L H J T I K L I K I E O O
E N U K L M N A H M I H E R C A R T N H D D
N O R T H D A K O T A N A G L B N I D U A E
S R I R U O S S I M I T A I S A A S I K R I
N E W H A M P S H I R E B N O M O R A E O S
X G T P P I S S I S S I M I V A V W N S L L
Y O C I X E M W E N D E L A W A R E A Z O A
X N I S N O C S I W R T S A N A T N O M C N
T T U C I T C E N N O C S I O N I L L I X D
```

MONTHS OF THE YEAR PUZZLE

Contained in this square are the months of the year. They can be read up, down, backward, and diagonally. For answer see page 76.

```
J U B E R D E C A N U R Y J U L I E
S A U V E D A Y S T E L Y E W S P N
R P D E C E N T A Y M R A B C U M E
E R B U V R E B S L A I L A R P A L
B O N O V E R T O U R M A R T Y W N
M L E R S O P C R J C J A N U I E R
E T C B E R T B O T H A P R I O T S
C S I P E O E O U J A U N T S R E B
E A S O B F A Y R A U N A J A P O T
D Y M E R S T E M B E N O P T M T A
A P R I T E B S O T U X E E U S O M
M A R C L M A R C K B C M E U A E L
J A N U E Y P A E R S B U G E V Y S
U O J V T R S E P T E M U R O A E R
M Y O S M A M L I R P A E N J U L A
E N U N E A T R S B E S E P T E M S
S Y A N T O S P Y O C T O P B E A E
L E D E C E N B E T J U N A L Y T R
```

DAYS OF THE WEEK PUZZLE

Harry Wilson

Contained in this square are the days of the week. For answer see page 76.

```
M O N D Y T H U Y E R S A Y
O T F R I A Y A D S A T E R
N H T U E S D T M O T D A Y
T U A F R R H S A U R M O N
D R I A U U S U E S A T I T
A E Y T R D A S U N D A R U
T P A S E C D N F O D R S E
A S D N O A D A Y O T E R S
T A I S Y A D N O M O N W T
Y A R D Y F R I L A Y O T A
R S F R I D A L O M P C B Y
J U A R L Y E S F R I D A T
S A T T I S U N T A Y T H O
M O N T U E S D P T S A T F
```

PENCIL PUZZLE

By drawing four straight lines, can you connect all nine points of the diamond—without lifting your pencil from the paper, and without retracing any lines?

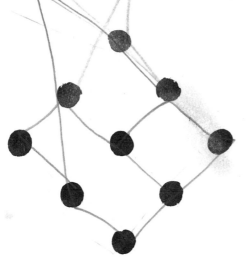

ANSWER

The solution may surprise you. If you have to peek, it's on page 76.

COLOR

A book title, song, magazine, flower, bird or writer.

Red	Yellow
Blue	Pink
Green	Purple
White	Gray
Black	Orange

Suggested answers on page 77.

ANNE GOUGLER

DETAILS

How much attention do you pay to details? Try to reconstruct the order of houses on your street, stores where you go most often, or names of hotels you know are near each other? Do you remember the details of what your last visitor was wearing? Or what you had for dinner two days ago?

HOW WELL DO YOU REASON?

About one third of all high-school seniors who seek college admission take the College Entrance Examination Board's three-hour Scholastic Aptitude Test. This is a specialized form of what is usually called an intelligence test or mental-ability test. Its questions are not designed to find out how much you know, but rather to test your thinking ability, your capacity to deal with ideas and problems, so that predictions may be ventured about your future success in academic work.

Below are questions similar to those asked in the so-called "verbal" sections of the Scholastic Aptitude Test. To check yourself against what is expected of today's college applicants, follow the directions for each section. Then see the answers on page 77.

SENTENCE COMPLETIONS: These questions test comprehension of sentence meaning. Each sentence below has one or more blank spaces, each of which indicates that a word has been omitted. Choose the word or pair of words which, when inserted in the blank spaces, best fits the meaning of the sentence.

1. If your garden plot is small, it will not pay to grow crops which require a large amount of——— in order to develop.

(A) moisture (B) rain (C) fertilizer (D) space (E) care.

2. The American colonies were separate and —— entities, each having its own government and being entirely ——.

(A) incomplete . . . revolutionary (B) independent . . . interrelated (C) unified . . . competitive (D) growing . . . organized (E) distinct . . . independent.

3. Iron rusts from ——, stagnant water loses its purity; even so does —— sap the vigor of the mind.

(A) disuse . . . inaction (B) abuse . . . delinquency (C) misuse . . . imitation (D) acid . . . alcohol (E) age . . . misuse.

4. Since growth is not a —— process for all people, the importance of studying the —— growth pattern has been emphasized.

(A) uniform . . . individual (B) healthy . . . normal (C) unique . . . varying (D) simple . . . fundamental (E) normal . . . typical.

5. If we cannot make the wind blow when and where we wish it to blow, we can at least make use of its ——.

(A) source (B) heat (C) aroma (D) force (E) atmosphere.

ANALOGIES: The questions below test your sensitivity to relationships among words and ideas. Each question consists of two words which bear a certain relationship to each other, followed by five other pairs of related words. From the five others (A, B, C, D and E) select the pair which are related in the *same* way as the key pair.

1. Borderland:County—(A) water:land (B) rock:soil (C) margin:page (D) danger:safety (E) shelf:edge.

2. Tree:Forest—(A) flower:plant (B) chair:room (C) cloth:fiber (D) voice:chorus (E) mistake:life.

3. Grove:Tree—(A) monastery:monk (B) pond:stream (C) illumination:watt (D) peninsula:isthmus (E) archipelago:island.

4. Lamps:Darkness—(A) books:ignorance (B) books:publication (C) books:fame (D) ignorance:fame (E) publication:fame.

5. Ointment:Burn—(A) water:fire (B) sympathy:sorrow (C) medicine:doctor (D) powder:face (E) pain:agony.

6. Calamity:Distress—(A) tidings:jubilation (B) triumph:exultation (C) emergency:desolation (D) news:gratification (E) war:victory.

7. Trigger:Bullet—(A)handle:drawer (B) holster:gun (C) bulb:light (D) switch:current (E) pulley:rope.

See page 77 for answers to quiz.

YOUR LITERARY I. Q.

CONfused?

"While CONfined at Ohio Penitentiary in Columbus," writes Don Long, "I compiled this list of words, each of which includes the letter combination CON. If your readers CONcentrate they might furnish the missing letters without using their lexiCONS." Answers on page 77.

1. _ _ _ CON	watchtower
2. _ CON _ _ _ _ _	he watches expenses
3. _ _ _ CON	hawk
4. _ CON _ _ _ _ _	attacks beliefs
5. _ _ _ CON	church worker
6. _ _ _ CON	boaster
7. _ _ _ CON _ _ _ _ _	interpret wrongly
8. CON _ _ _ _	disapprove
9. _ _ _ CON _ _ _ _ _ _	rebel
10. _ _ _ CON _	depart clandestinely
11. _ _ CON _ _ _ _ _	unaware
12. _ _ _ CON	inexpensive stone
13. _ _ _ _ CON _ _ _ _ _ _	excessively self-assured
14. _ _ CON _ _ _ _ _	observe or scout
15. _ _ CON _ _ _ _	storyteller

JOHN T. WINTERICH

NAME TEN OF EACH

1. Composer
2. Kinds of fur
3. Fish
4. Writers
5. Bodies of water
6. Flowers
7. Articles of clothing
8. Best friends
9. Operas
10. Book titles
11. Food for breakfast
12. Food for lunch
13. Food for dinner
14. Titles of poems
15. Counties in your state
16. Favorite actors
17. Favorite movies
18. Trees
19. Adages
20. Rivers

Answers on pages 77–78.

HIDDEN WORDS

Category	
Flower	M E T A N I P R Z U K I
Bird	B R E A L U G K E M
Color	K N R B E R R U L
Vegetable	H U A D E S M I D Z R
Tree	S L U D E X M A P
Fruit	A Z O M R T P S U L
Girl's name	V P L N I T A Z Y S
Boy's name	S L E R U T O K E B R

Page 78 has the answers.

LISTEN, LISTEN

Listen intently and write down twelve different sounds you can hear.

INVENTIONS

If you were an inventor what five things would you invent for a patient in the hospital?

NOT FOUND ON A DESERT ISLAND

Between breakfast and lunch a person needs twenty different items not to be found on a desert island. Name them. Page 78 has some suggested answers.

ANNE GOUGLER

INFORMATION DESK

Facts from here and there add interest and may increase your fund of knowledge. See page 78 for answer.

GEORGE W. FRANK

ACROSS

1 Wild dog
7 Cold dish
12 Coat part
16 Fresh-water protozoan
17 Type of jewel
18 Formerly
19 Frankfurter
20 Acknowledge
21 Asian designation, in part
22 Theological degree
23 Horseshoeing frame
25 English letter
27 Coarse fabric
28 Roman date
29 Desert phenomenon
31 Bath, for one
34 Selves
35 Robert E. Lee's horse
37 Satellite instruments
39 Participated
40 Kind of show
41 Application form
42 Adage
45 Gathers in
46 Whim
47 Island near Naples
49 Part of a house
50 Board
51 Sportsman of a kind
52 Thoroughgoing
54 Morning event
55 Encircle
58 Shape of some hats
59 Scatter new-mown hay
60 Cheerful
61 Ducks' milieu
62 No matter what one
63 Baste
65 Science of reasoning
67 Fabric on a loom
70 Storm
72 Twangy
74 Architectural feature
76 Shank
77 Hoisting machine
78 Power scoop-shovel
79 Fowl
80 Bordered
81 Time of growth

DOWN

1 Parts of a vise
2 Pierrot and others
3 Prom girl
4 Understanding: Scot.
5 Sanction
6 Oil-tanned moccasin
7 Barrel strips
8 Assistants
9 Book of the Bible: Abbr.
10 State: Abbr.
11 Manufacturer's rubber stamp
12 Mazel ____
13 Ark passenger
14 Period of geological time
15 Athlete's award
24 Fusses
26 Swan or swallow

30 Man's nickname
31 Twenty
32 Section of fence
33 Make ____ of
34 Stages of history
35 Express gratitude
36 Station
38 Ruler: Abbr.
39 Personal attitude
41 Trademark
42 Cut lengthwise
43 Came into being
44 Ready for sound transmission
46 Social group
47 Bamboo's cousin
48 Ventilate
50 Wisdom

51 Time instruments
52 College course
53 Sea food
54 Madrigal
55 Explore
56 Third carpal bone
57 Weapon of future
58 Lost intensity
61 Smoothing tool
64 Division of a city
66 Harvest
67 Bed of a stream, dry at times
68 Utopia's relative
69 Icy mass
71 Letter
73 Droop
75 Diner

34

CHANGE OF FACE

Diagramless style patterning, for a change, but the same process of filling
in those words. See page 78 for answer.

WALTER WELLMAN

ACROSS

1 Kind of bean
4 Young pigeon
6 Endure
10 Treated with disdain
12 Tags
16 Plant of the lily family
17 Suggestion
18 Explorer Tasman
19 Beginning
20 Succor
21 Day of rest: Abbr.
22 Greek letter
23 Boston, for one
25 Valuable grass
27 Seasons
29 Dwindle (with "out")
30 "Bolero" man
33 Cooking direction
35 Pry
39 Separated
41 Inlet
42 Added up
44 When the alarm rings
45 Atavism
48 Positive "no!"
50 Distant
51 Misstatement
52 Shooter, in marbles
53 Measure (out)
54 Retard
56 Loosened
59 Flat hat
60 Costumes
62 Pronoun
63 Part of the kitchen sink
65 Relinquish office
66 Article of faith
68 Potential babysitters
69 Radii, for example
71 Grades
73 Activated
76 Assembly
80 Aroma
81 Taste
83 Resort
84 Sewing basket
85 Spanish pot
86 Kitchen appliance
88 Strip of shoe leather
89 Ship: Poet.
90 Beaus
91 Otherwise
92 Cookies
93 Three, in Spain

DOWN

1 Cuttlefish
2 Pronoun: Dial.
3 Jerks
4 Fairies
5 Retarded
6 Lingers
7 Nautical term
8 Rail
9 Enticed
10 Fairway
11 Bookkeeper's concern
12 Little stand
13 Help
14 Meg's sister
15 Kill
24 Machinist's helper
26 Juicy fruit
28 Yells
29 Mason
30 Competed (with)
31 Mean
32 Sommelier's specialty
34 Tune
36 Large truck
37 Ingredient
38 Regards highly
39 Put off
40 Perry Mason's aide
42 Pulled along
43 Discourage
44 Deplorable
46 Roman road
47 Man's name
49 Inactive: Abbr.
55 Edible root
56 Squelch
57 Knowledge: Scot.
58 Male duck
59 Crib
61 Broad-minded
64 Harsh
66 Wearisome
67 Meddles (with)
70 Cozy abodes
72 Comes close
73 Peer
74 Inactive
75 Field mouse
77 Type of type: Abbr.
78 Parochial school
    teachers
79 French writer
82 Grease ——
83 Mining term
87 Arcturus

GETTING THE PICTURE

Here's a gallery of words which the 26 Across will find of particular interest. See page 78 for answer.

JOSEPH CROWELL

ACROSS

1 Trojan prince
6 Domino
10 Legal document
14 Ad ____
17 Queen: Fr.
18 Project
19 California fish
20 Kind of castle
21 Clubs
22 Void's partner
23 Consort of Edward II of England
25 Prods
26 Art ____
28 Home of a sort
29 Poetic contraction
30 Genoa, for one
31 Anchorite
33 Manifestations
35 On the qui vive
37 Site of ancient Panhellenic games
41 Government official
43 Beatitude
44 Colorful birds
45 They say: Fr.
46 Lures
47 Bestow
48 Common verb form
49 Snow leopard
50 "September ____"
51 Truth, in China
52 Famous Boston art center
56 ____ glance
59 Newsstand buys, for short
60 Made public
61 Relative of a transept
65 Attractive to buyers
67 Suffix with home or farm
68 Like some Bostonians
69 Catch onto: Colloq.
70 West ____
71 Shade of blue
72 "____ of Two Cities"
73 Rich clays
74 Open
75 Confirm
77 Prefix with drome or dynamics
78 Crest
81 Isaac's son
84 Left Bank feature
87 Artist's skill
88 What art is
90 Take down ____
91 Table: Lat.
92 Inhabitant: Abbr.
93 Dossier
94 Musical instrument
95 Provoke
96 Greek letter
97 Helper: Abbr.
98 Leaf cutters
99 Flavorful

DOWN

1 Vainglory
2 Bird's home
3 Matamoros's waterway
4 Auberges
5 His: Fr.
6 Youths
7 Grown
8 Market
9 Vegetable
10 Members of PEN
11 Holiday haven
12 Embrace
13 Check
14 Robust
15 Pictures
16 Suffix with pluto or demo
24 Matriculates
26 Newcastle product
27 Game of skill
30 Danube tributary
32 Artless: Fr.
34 Wielding
35 ____ blue
36 Letter for letter
38 Greet
39 Sight from Taormina
40 About
41 Male swan
42 Type of armed bandit
43 Public announcements
44 Slipped
46 Move
47 Sat
49 Fanon
50 Spouse of Caroline Bonaparte
53 Walks easily
54 Bearings
55 Mother: Prefix
56 Fictional canine
57 Tense
58 Girl's name
62 Works of art
63 1 Down, for one
64 Dutch commune
66 Patterned change in vowels, as sing, sang, sung
67 Foot parts
68 Starch
70 Hen
71 Grouper, a fish
73 Certain works of art
74 Soft colors
76 Oriental garments
77 Expert
79 Beginning
80 Famous explorer
81 ____ homo!
82 Please
83 High: Lat.
85 Bark cloth
86 ____ arms
87 River of Asia
89 Bashkir city
91 Picture framer's item

UTOPIAS

Utopia is our prize contribution to pencil pleasures in Paradise. You take a word you don't like and change it into something you do by altering one letter at a time.

For instance, you can go from NUTS to SANE in six moves—NUTS, GUTS, GATS, GATE, LATE, LANE, SANE—but if you try to go from BALMY to LUCID even in twenty moves you'll be right back where you started from.

We never did get from INTERN to DOCTOR, WRONG to RIGHT, DUNCE to SMART, FIGHT to PEACE, NURSE to BRIDE, WORKINGMAN to CAPITALIST, MALADY to HEALTH, though after a week of trying we finally got from BROKEN to MENDED.

Here are some Utopias the answers of which are on pages 78–79. The lines below them indicate the number of changes it took us to get from something bad to something good. You may be astute enough to make the transitions in half the changes. If you do, it shows you're twice as bright as we are—something both of us suspected from the beginning.

UTOPIAS

Dark to Dawn

Low to Top

Wan to Fun

Vale to Hill

Boy to Man

Awake to Smoke

Wet to Dry

Sick to Jake

Cat to Dog

Coma to Talk

Dolt to Sage

Hurt to Well

Drain to Dried

Walk to Jump

Near to Fame

Fear to None

Temp to Norm

Broken to Mended

FRANK SCULLY

Nellie Nifty, R.N.

*"It's wonderful having a doctor who
can't say 'It's all in your mind.'"*

Cartoon by KAZ, © 1967 by *Modern Medicine.*

"You made it!"

Cartoon by KAZ, © 1965 by *Modern Medicine.*

ACT III *Department of Labor*

Checking into a hospital for maternity is an experience no man can really relate or relate to. And until modern science advances a good bit farther than it already has, it remains an exclusively feminine affair.

It should be a happy one, too—full of terrific excitement in spite of the apprehension, the pain and the uncertainty—because it carries the promise of relief, the end of a long wait, as well as answers to the questions Boy or girl? One or twins? Resemble Mama or Papa?

A woman in labor often acts intoxicated, which she is, in a sense. But not from the usual causes. Her intoxication is a volatile mixture of wild anticipation and good old fear.

Having checked in and been tucked into bed, anticlimax sometimes sets in. Things often bog down. There is a tedious, nervous and pain-filled wait. Sure, it won't be long (you hope) until the new baby appears on the scene, and that will be a joy, but during labor all this seems far from reality. The only thing real is the agony and the boredom and the slowness of it all.

How to spend this irksome interim? Why not turn to the Game Preserve section for escape?

Later, after you return to civilian life, you can go back and do the games over again—correctly this time.

We all know that the first human act a baby encounters in this world is a big whack, so he can cry and thereby fill his lungs with air.

Along came a baby who didn't cry. He laughed. No matter what anyone did to him he laughed. And his fist was closed tight. This was rather unusual. The doctor tried various ways to open it. Finally he managed, and there in the palm of the baby's hand was

THE PILL.

A new father, after pacing the corridors of the maternity sanitarium for hours, was finally given the news. It was a girl.

"Thank God," he said piously. "I'd never want a son of mine to go through what I have today."

FRANCIS LEO GOLDEN

"Are you sure you want to go through with this, dear?"

Cartoon by Davie, © 1966 by *Modern Medicine.*

HIGHLY SPECIALIZED

During a discussion of movies one evening, I asked a young doctor if all those many pots of boiling water that country doctors on the screen invariably ask for are really necessary in delivering a baby at home.

"I wondered about that myself, because the only boiling water you really need is a very small panful for your hypo," the physician replied. "But one of my medical school professors who had been a country doctor for many years gave a good explanation. 'If you ever deliver a baby at home, the thing that will give you the most trouble will be the expectant father,' he warned us in a lecture. 'He'll be so nervous that he'll continually pester you and be under foot unless you give him something to do. Tell him you'll need lots of hot water. Most farmhouses have coal or wood stoves, and keeping the fire hot and the water boiling will get the father out of your way. After it's all over and you tell him the glad tidings, why you and he have the makings for some steaming hot coffee!' "

Mrs. T. R. Weiss

"After this, nurse, bring out just *one baby at a time!"*

Cartoon by Reamer Keller, © 1966 by Adcox Associates, Inc.

The obstetrician made his way through the country lane to deliver the ninth baby of a backwoods (but scarcely backward) couple. A duck scooted across the doctor's pathway.

"Just a duck," said the husband, who came forward as a guide.

"A duck, eh? For a moment I thought it was the stork with his legs worn down."

Francis Leo Golden

EXPLANATION-WISE

Jack Paar asked Frank Scully, father of five, why he had so many children. "Because," said Frank, "we never wanted the youngest one to be spoiled!"

Earl Wilson

CELEBRANT

Cartoon by DAVID LANGDON, © 1968 by Cowles Communications, Inc.

Two fathers were pacing up and down the fathers' room. Finally the nurse came in with a little bundle, a brown baby face sticking out of the blanket.

"Is this your baby?" she asked one man. He rather disdainfully denied any connection with the baby.

"Well, then it must be yours," the nurse said cheerfully to the other man, "you're the only other man here."

He looked at the baby, thought a bit, looked again and then said, "Yes, I guess it could be mine. My wife burns everything."

☙❧

BABYTALK, FROM PARIS TO HOLLYWOOD

Our first child was born in Paris.

Having a baby in France was a delightful experience. Everybody had the attitude that any woman having a child was doing the country a service. Seemingly she could do no wrong. George Canty, U.S. Trade Commissioner to France, told us that French drivers were so terrible he never dared cross a street until he could find a pregnant woman to accompany him. He was right. On the Champs Elysées, where the street is at least eight lanes wide, traffic came to a standstill whenever I crossed, no matter how wrong I was in choosing the spot.

Once while walking down a crowded boulevard I passed two young men. They greeted me with a gallant and flirtatious *Bon jour.* There was a pause as they noticed my condition, and charmingly added, *"Maman."*

The reverse side of all this tender loving care for prospective mothers was all the old wives' tales they would spin about the effects of prenatal impressions. One mother urged me to feast my eyes on her children, who she felt were the most gorgeous on earth, so that my child, too, would be beautiful. Others warned about bending, stretching, sweeping with a broom or walking up stairs, but recommended going to operas, concerts and museums. I had to remind myself that women also had babies in China and in Greenland, where the rules were different, and somehow most of the chil-

"Does it cry and talk like mine?"

Cartoon by M. GIUFFRE, © 1967 by Parade Publications, Inc.

"At least we have each other, Prince."

Cartoon by M. GIUFFRE, © 1967 by Parade Publications, Inc.

dren were born healthy. So I just went on living, and doing my chores around the house. One thing did bother me though, and that was the Manx cat. This is a breed that has no tail. How come? Could it have been an accidental lopping off somewhere in its past history? I felt it was too silly to ask about it, but it terrified me nevertheless because Frank, my husband, the father of my child, had had his one leg amputated a few years earlier, after about seventeen operations, to control osteomyelitis. (This infection now takes about a week of penicillin to cure.) It became a thing with me, but I kept it to myself.

When it was time, I went to the American Hospital in Paris. It had a school for nurses, and it so happened that over half of the students were young Norwegian girls, many of whom I had gone to school with in first and second grades in Norway.

I lay there in the labor room, young, inexperienced and scared out of my wits remembering those somber tales, a heritage of the dark ages, which had been poured into me.

The doctor came and went. He checked me over, felt on the outside and said, "There's one foot." At that moment a young nurse stuck her head in the door and said, "Doctor, telephone." He was out the door before I could ask, "Where's the other?" I never saw him again till hours later after the baby was born.

The news of my presence had spread like wildfire among the students. By the time I got to the delivery room eight of my former classmates came in along with the obstetrical crew, all of whom were quite annoyed with our babbling in a language they didn't understand. Everyone was there except the doctor, who insisted on finishing his dessert. The nurses gave me little whiffs of gas, trying to delay the birth till the doctor's arrival. One pretty girl standing there holding my hand said, "I really shouldn't be here. I'm on duty in isolation."

A new fear struck me. Would my child be born with diphtheria, whooping cough and scarlet fever, maybe even leprosy, all at once?

Finally the baby made his appearance.

"Has he got two legs?" I asked.

The room rocked with laughter. Never having seen Frank, they didn't know the reason for my fear. But they reassured me.

"He has enormous feet," one girl volunteered. "He's going to be a giant."

"And a big head," another one said. "You know, if he were mine, I think I'd throw him out and start all over again," she added kiddingly.

I took a look at him. He was no beauty I thought, and, lapsing into English, I said so, as I commented on the fact that his head was so big his shoulders didn't even go out as far as his ears. "He looks like a little old wrinkled man," I added. Since much of the kidding had been in Norwegian, the regular ob nurse must have failed to sense my love for "that wrinkled little old man." A couple of hours later, back in my room, the supervisor and another nurse came around and talked me into "keeping him." As if I had ever thought otherwise.

Finally the day arrived for us to leave the hospital. Until we could take the long train trip back to the Riviera, where we lived at that time, home for the next couple of weeks was a hotel.

The hotel was a charming place to stay while gaining strength and getting acquainted with Skip. We had big French windows opening onto a lovely sunlit garden below and our favorite outdoor restaurant. I had no problem with formulas, as I was nursing my baby.

The chambermaids were wonderful. Whenever I had to go out for a meal or on an errand I would notify the maid. Not only she, but the maids from the other floors and the manager's wife, congregated in my room to take turns rocking the baby. The baby learned quickly. The minute he heard my door close he would set up a wail for all these beautiful Frenchwomen to come to his aid. And that they did. When about an hour later he heard my voice thanking them, he shut up like a clam. The fun was over for the day.

The man in the next room, who had lived there for twelve years, complained that the baby at times cried during the night. It did happen. Skip wasn't adjusted yet to the cruel, cold world. The manager turned a deaf ear. "What did you do when you were a baby?" he asked.

They finally compromised. They placed a mattress up against the door connecting the rooms. Not on my side, mind you, but on his. "Mother and child must not be disturbed."

Between the time I had my first baby in Paris and my fourth in Hollywood, all fears and superstitions were swept away, and with it also the gallantry which had made pregnancy and motherhood in France such an exciting event.

We were down to the prosaic worrying about the difficulty of getting to the hospital on time. We had just recently moved into a new house on top of a hill overlooking Hollywood, and I was the only chauffeur in the family. The roads were winding and narrow, and Frank had great doubts as to a taxi ever finding the place on a dark night. He was absolutely sure the baby would arrive during the night, for hadn't all the others done it? What was so exceptional about this one, so far?

Hollywood friends like director John Ford, author Jim Tully and actor Bill Harrigan volunteered to be on call. Frank settled on Bill since he lived at the Montecito, an apartment house right below us. Even though it was a tall building we looked down on its roof terrace from our house. The road leading to it was quite circuitous. When we finally did put through the call for Bill, it was, of course, four A.M.

"Could you take me to the hospital, Bill?"

Instead of solid reassurance, there was a long silence and a groan. "I just got to bed. I was at a big party. Couldn't you wait a bit?"

"I don't think so, Bill. I already waited over an hour to call you, so you could get some more sleep."

"It would have been better then," he said. "I was still up an hour ago."

There was some more groaning. "I tell you," said Bill, "why don't you drive down and pick me up, and I'll take over from here?"

Frank and I looked at each other. "Sure, Bill. That'll be okay." After all, I felt he was putting himself out to help me, so why shouldn't I be accommodating?

So Frank and I got in our car, Frank with his hand on the brake—just in case—as I wedged in behind the steering wheel. When we arrived at the Montecito, there stood Bill and his wife, Grace, in the shivering predawn. Grace felt she was needed for moral support—if not for me, at least for Bill, who was quite unnerved by the whole idea. They crawled into the back seat while he asked if I couldn't possibly drive as far as the drive-in at Sunset and Vine for a reassuring cup of coffee.

I surveyed the situation. Traffic was light, and I could make the ten or twelve blocks hopefully without too many stops for the pains to pass. At the drive-in we ordered three cups of coffee. The thought of it was almost too much for me. But I felt I had to get my protectors into shape to protect me.

The coffee didn't work too well. I knew there wasn't time for another round, so I started driving down Sunset Boulevard. Every few blocks I would pull over to the curb until the labor pain had passed, and then set out again. My "chauffeur" felt I was doing fine. I drove to the hospital.

By the time we entered the hospital, dawn was breaking. I was so relieved that I suddenly realized the idiocy of the whole situation and became slightly hysterical.

I was led to the elevator. Frank was told to take a seat in the fathers' room and wait for about forty-five minutes, when he would be able to come into my room and stay with me. I felt this was silly at that hour of the morning and told him to go home. Knowing that Bill and Grace were waiting downstairs, he didn't protest, but he noticed a red-eyed, worried father pacing up and down. He asked him how long the doctor had told him he still had to wait? "About eight hours," he said. "Okay," said Frank. "Why don't you pace for me too? I'll call you every once in a while. Meanwhile I'll go home to bed." The guy was astounded at such cool but said okay. Every few hours Frank would call and get progress reports on both mamas.

I had plenty of time to reflect on the differences between France, when my first baby was so gently ushered into the world, and now, when I had to be a flunkey to my flunkeys.

I remembered how, in order for Skip to be an American citizen, I had to go to the consulate and register him before the fortieth day. (This was a reciprocity agreement with France.) On the thirty-ninth day I set out for downtown Paris to do just that. Frank couldn't do it, for while I was in the hospital he had dislocated his hip and was then in the hospital himself.

On coming out of the consulate I tried to get a taxi. They were all lined up but no driver would look my way, or even answer when spoken to. It seems we were approaching zero hour of the beginning of the Tour de France, a bicycle race around France, an event as exciting to the French as the World Series is to us. I finally crossed over to a gendarme and complained. He explained that I couldn't expect anybody to take me home till the race was under way. "Just be patient," he said, "in another hour you can get a taxi easily."

"But," I said, "I have a baby at home, and I must get home to nurse him."

He cross-questioned me to make sure that I was telling the truth. Then French gallantry took over. "Hey you, take this lady home, she has a baby who needs to be nursed."

The taxi driver argued and hollered. But the policeman was adamant. The taxi driver wavered between wishing that I was lying, and Gallic chivalry. It was killing him. He finally buckled, opened the door for me, and lit out as only French taxi drivers can. At every stop and traffic light he leaned out the window to tell the world about the terrible injustice that befell him, he who had a front seat for the Tour de France. As often as possible people would make way to let him through. After all, who were they to obstruct traffic for a mother rushing home to nurse her infant?

Steady pains brought me back to the labor room in a Hollywood hospital, and concern about how this baby would turn out. As far as we the parents were concerned, of course, all we wanted was a healthy baby. But the children? Skip, now a little American boy so anxious for a baby brother, after two sisters, had several times told me, "Mom, next time, don't let's take a chance, let's adopt a boy."

The baby turned out to be another girl. "A lovely, healthy baby," the doctor assured me. But on his next visit an hour or so later he seemed unusually solicitous and even comforting. I became alarmed. Was there something wrong with the baby? No, the baby was fine, I was assured. I couldn't figure out his unusual behavior, and he volunteered nothing.

When he left I called Frank. With a big laugh he explained that when the doctor called him to report the arrival of another daughter, Skip had rushed to answer the phone, so the doctor told him he had a little sister.

Skip, no gallant Frenchman he, had ordered a brother. On hearing the turn of events, he had abruptly hung up the phone.

ALICE SCULLY

"Congratulations, it's a baby!"

Cartoon by Lundberg, © 1965 by McNaught Syndicate, Inc.

"What I'm going to say now is off the record."

Cartoon by Doris Mathews, © 1965 by Saturday Review, Inc.

*"I was wondering, Dr. Maxby, in an effort
to save me time, if I could have copies
of your notes for my biographer."*

Cartoon by H. Martin, © 1966 by Saturday Review, Inc.

ACT IV

It's All in Your Mind

If your drive has gotten up and driven away,
If you just can't face those bills you must pay,
If you're feeling disturbed and distressed,
Can't get up in the morning and get dressed,
And you've turned to this section in your grief,
Its title prescribes your relief,
So put all your worries behind,
For in fact—

IT'S ALL IN YOUR MIND!

BOB LANE

Cartoon by SCHULZ, © 1968 by United Features Syndicate, Inc.

47

A PATIENT NEEDS AN AUDIENCE, DOC

One thing leads to another. That's the story. If there had never been a first thing, nothing would have followed. Not long ago Dr. Vladimir K. Zworykin was issued Patent No. 3,215,848 for a photosensitive information retrieval device to be used for medical electronics.

There are 10,000 known diseases and each one may have 600 or more symptoms. The symptoms of each disease are stored in the memory cells of the computer.

A patient comes to a doctor and tells his or her symptoms, which are fed into the computer and out pops a card telling what the sickness is. This would allow the doctor to be an illiterate howler monkey or a fiddler crab.

A succeeding computer will undoubtedly follow to diagnose and to suggest treatment—no more bedside manner, no more witchcraft or chronic and communicable hypochondria and, worst of all, no more errors.

It's a horrible thing to contemplate, don't you think? It occurs to me to hope that no humor cells are grafted into this machine, otherwise there might be some critical comment not entirely flattering to the patient, like "You're too fat!" or "Who do you think you're kidding?"

Malingering is not limited to the armed services. Some people will pay a lot of money to lie to a doctor.

During the war my partner Ed Richetts was a laboratory assistant at the induction and basic training center at Fort Ord in California. One day a cherub in ODs came in. "Doc," he said, "I been bit by a rattlesnake. I need a drink of whiskey bad."

Ed replied, "In these cases it is customary for the doctor to drink the whiskey to steel himself so he can shove a horse syringe of anti-venom into the victim's hide. O.K., let's see the bite!"

The boy held up his wrist, and Ed saw four definite punctures, oozing a little blood. Ed sighed. "Son," he said, "I'm going to give you a shot of whiskey so you can stand the shock of what I have to tell you."

"Is it bad, Doc?"

"Just awful," said Richetts. "A rattlesnake only has two fangs. This one obviously struck, did a flip-flop and hit again." He poured a hooker of his own whiskey for the boy. "Son," he said, "next time you get took sick, do a little reading."

Maybe this new computer will make reading unnecessary except by the man who makes computers. But that's only a lead into what I want to tell you. This device gives me an idea which will make my fortune, if it doesn't get me killed. Maybe you might like to put some money in my invention.

A lot of my friends go to psychoanalysts. The doctor is so busy that he has to charge astronomic prices for listening to these couch fruits. With my invention, one analyst could turn on thirty or forty patients at once. They would lie in cubicles each with his or her own photosensitive information retrieval device.

I can hear your objections before you voice them, and I have plugged the holes you anticipate. If the patient stops talking, a tape will say in a soothing, ultra-lateral voice, "Yes, just so, and then what did you think, say, do, dream?" Or, "You dropped off. Wake up, sir, madam!"

I know there are several schools of psychoanalysis, and that is taken care of. A switch can be twisted to Freud, Jung, Adler, or All my own work.

Your next objection will be "How are you going to take care of the contingent dangers? Doesn't the patient at one time or another fall in love with the doctor?"

"I've thought of that. You remember the rubber Lincoln at the World's Fair. Why should a patient have to fall in love with a bald, pot-bellied gargoyle with a middle-European accent, when there is a choice of Kirk Douglas, Frank Sinatra, Mayor John Lindsay or, in unusual cases, General de Gaulle in lifelike automated rubber in which the computer is installed. Husbands and wives of patients would like this method better, too.

The owner or, better, renter of my devices could raise his prices and take all the patients available or drop the prices and break the market. In any case, we patent holders would get ours.

The head shrinker would have a choice, too. He could either go over the results and evaluate them or pay a little more money for a second device, much better informed, which would make the diagnosis and suggest the cure.

And again, we can only hope that the machines do not develop within themselves a diabolic trait foreign to both doctor and patients—a sense of humor. That would ruin the pitch.

Darn it, I had forgot one thing and it blows the whole deal. I had overlooked the cast-iron pediment of psychoanalytic popularity. The patient needs an audience, demands an audience, is willing to pay through the nose for someone to bore.

Maybe they wouldn't be content to spill over to Kirk Douglas, even in living, automated rubber. There's always a flaw. You know, for a little while I thought I had it made.

JOHN STEINBECK

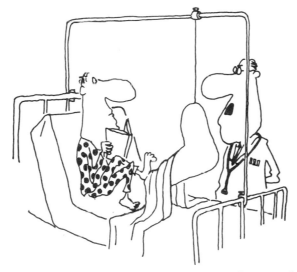

"You cannot receive the benefits of modern medical science unless you cooperate, Mr. Jones."

Cartoon by MAO, © 1907 by *Modern Medicine.*

"Is it contagious?"

Cartoon by D. GERARD, © 1967 by Parade Publications, Inc.

ID BITS

Overheard in a psychiatrist's waiting room: "I can't help it, doctor. I keep thinking my inferiority complex is bigger and better than anybody else's."

MIKE CONNOLLY

At the State Mental Hospital at Marlboro, New Jersey, one of the newer members of the psychiatric staff was accosted by a patient: "We like you better than the last doctor who was here."

The psychiatrist was elated. "I'm happy to hear it."

"Yeah," continued the patient, "you seem more like one of us."

FRANCIS LEO GOLDEN

A psychiatrist, drawing pictures, asks his patient what they make him think of. First he draws a square. The patient looks at it and gives a long explanation involving sex.

Then he draws a circle. The patient thinks this reminds him of a nude, voluptuous woman. The triangle also gets some connotation of that sort.

The psychiatrist exclaims, "Man, are you in trouble! All you think of is sex!"

Patient: "But you are the one who draws those dirty pictures."

The fashionable psychiatrist finished his notes and turned to the lady in front of him. "I'll be perfectly frank," he said. "I find nothing the matter—nothing abnormal—and I shall so inform your relatives."

"Thank you, Doctor, I was sure you'd say that," she replied. "I only came here to please my family. After all, there's nothing very strange about a fondness for pancakes, is there?"

"Pancakes?" repeated the psychiatrist. "Certainly not. I'm fond of them myself."

"Are you?" she queried brightly. "Then you must come over to my house. I have trunks full of them!"

STRANGE NEW WORLD

The floor nurse at the Latter-day Saints Hospital in Salt Lake City was trying to speak via the intercom to a patient in the children's ward. After receiving no answer from the child, she said, "Jimmy, I know you're there."

A few seconds later a tiny, quavering voice replied, "What do you want, wall?"

ONLY SICK PEOPLE
GO TO DOCTORS

I maintain that I can cure your hypochondria or at least demonstrate a dignified way of living with it. And I will brook no criticism—clinical or lay, AMA or Walgreen's—in my prescription for a short cut to getting rid of it simply by pointing up the kinship of identical symptoms and discomfitures and treating each with reverence and disdain. This is no more disquieting than your doctor's telling you, as my doctor did, that you are sound as a dollar, when you and de Gaulle know how sound the dollar really is.

One would think that after I had come safely through the years of physical and mental wear and tear of hypochondria I would now, twelve years later, be in gruesome disrepair. *Au contraire!* Physically I may be slightly impaired—those constant treks to doctors' offices can take their toll. But I'm all there mentally, having even developed at this late stage a remarkable total recall.

How about that for a new way of life—a *modus vivendi*—or, I should say, a *modus vivendi passato*. I can recall on a large screen and in color the slightest incident of the past, going as far back as those wonderful childhood days of yesteryear. It's the yesterdays I have most trouble with.

First you must understand that in treating hypochondria a physician is really helpless. There is nothing on which he can put his finger, like a pulse, or a doorbell. We have miracle drugs but we don't have miracle doctors. If you wander into a doctor's office with a series of intangible symptoms, he secretly wishes you had come in with a bad cough, which, as everyone knows, can be cured by a doctor in two weeks or without a doctor by lying abed fourteen days. A rule of thumb in the matter of medical advice is to take everything any doctor says with a grain of aspirin.

I cite case histories—mine. One doctor prescribed walking. "Walk to work every morning," he said. I did. My symptoms continued. True, my office is across the street from where I live. I hope he doesn't read this book.

Another doctor once fluoroscoped my heart and described it as "long and narrow." (That was the style they were wearing those days. Today I understand it's more heart-shaped.) In an attempt to mollify my fears he said, "If all the ailments in the world were hung out on a line to dry, you would choose your own." That miserable metaphoric prescription was no help. Actually he was wrong. I would have chosen lobar pneumonia compounded with a touch of pleurisy. That he could have handled.

One midnight when I realized I had cancer of the throat, a doctor came in answer to my emergency call and wiped it away with a piece of cotton on the end of a swab stick. Then he said, "Fill your tonsillectomy bag with ice and put it around your throat."

"Tonsillectomy bag?" I asked.

"You mean you don't have one?" he demanded.

I explained I didn't have room in my medicine cabinet for one, and he suggested warm drinks—some hot water with raspberry jam to make it palatable.

"Raspberry jam?" I asked.

Impatiently he went to the refrigerator and vainly searched for raspberry jam. If there was anyone not remotely prepared for this emergency it was I. He finally settled for grape jelly and had some on a slice of white bread.

Another one of my many doctors hit upon a plan. He said it was probably my teeth. I had been so busy being sick I hadn't been to a dentist in some time. I found a good one. He offered to rehabilitate my bite and promised a lifetime job; cost, thirty-five hundred dollars. It was worth it. I didn't feel much better, but I bit a lot better.

Two years later the rehabilitation started to fall apart. Back to the dentist.

"What happened to this lifetime job?" I sarcastically asked.

"Who knew you were going to live this long?" he replied petulantly.

GOODMAN ACE

WHAT A WAY TO GO

Winter blows around each windy corner now. ("Come to Jamaica!" say the warm ads in the slick magazines.) It is vitamin weather.

At least it *used* to be vitamin weather. Used to be I took vitamins in this kind of weather and felt fortified thereby. Then I read a piece in the health magazine:

"The use of vitamins is probably a harmless self-deception since our diets provide the small quantities needed daily."

The north wind doth blow and we shall have snow. I take good care of myself. I even spread margarine thinly. Wouldn't touch butter.

No, sir. The medics all said, "Butter and other animal fats are the major source of cholesterol." (I used to have to look up how to spell that. Now I just roll it off. Shows what concern can do to you.)

Anyway, I knocked off butter. Kept the old ticker ticking in waltz time.

Alas the health people now say it is not butter. It is sugar that sends you off. DOA on the hospital blotter. I've been pouring sugar down. Probably right now a mere shell.

For many years I gobbled carrots. I don't care much for carrots. But as every fool knows, they are a prime source of Vitamin A.

Eat carrots and you can see in the dark. See forever. That was the word when I ate carrots.

Attend now to the American Medical Association:

"More than half the people in the U.S. have eye

Nellie Nifty, R.N.

"Don't just stand there—cure me!"

Cartoon by KAZ, © 1967 by *Modern Medicine*.

"There's one *consolation—people will stop calling him a hypochondriac."*

Cartoon by KAZ, © 1965 by *Modern Medicine*.

trouble, but eating carrots will not improve their vision."

Oh, yes. I ate spinach, too. "It makes you good and strong. It is full of iron," said my family. I loathed it. But I ate it. Full of iron.

It turns out now it is also full of rocks. It can give you kidney stones. Good luck, Popeye the sailor ma-a-a-n!

If you eat olives and celery (by choice), chances are you have a higher than average IQ. You are a brain.

If you eat grapefruit, too, you're a genius. Maybe. Anyway, you were not behind the door when the brains were passed out.

This is the latest discovery by Science after a long and happy study of olive and celery and grapefruit eaters. (In my opinion, people who eat these things are merely hungry people. Some people can wait for the first course. Others are in there, snacking up the olives and celery. No control.)

On these brisk and invigorating mornings, I go out and pick up the paper and take several deep, healthy breaths.

We *all* know we don't breathe deep enough, right?

Wrong. An Army doctor has written a learned piece. Overbreathing can ruin you, man. It will cause you "dizziness, sensations of numbness, tingling, weakness, pain and muscle spasm," man.

So don't do it, man. Quit breathing.

Thus the scientists blow down my dream scatters. Make me stop self-deception—and I was a gay deceiver. Happy as could be.

Made me stop sweetening the coffee. Carrots? Forget it! Look back on a wasted rocky life of spinach. And almost convinced me to stop breathing. At least not gulp it in.

Even the smoky meat of the barbecue—(and that's Nature in the near raw)—is suspect. (Farewell to cookouts!) It seems the outside charred part does something dreadful to laboratory mice.

STAN DELAPLANE

GOOD BEHAVIOR

Cartoon by VIRGIL PARTCH, © 1966 by Cowles Communications, Inc.

MILESTONES IN MEDICINE

Hospitals 293 B.C.

When, in 293 B.C., the Roman gods seemed powerless to control a grave infectious disease which had broken out, a messenger was sent to the Greeks to borrow one of their gods, and for him the temple of Aesculapius was erected. At first, sick people came to the temple for religious reasons, but the Emperor Claudius, in 41 A.D., turned the temple into a place of refuge for poor people who were ill. The temple became a crude sort of hospital. As the Roman Empire extended over wider territory, other hospitals were erected at convenient places. With the rise of Christianity, Fabiola created her hospital where free care was given as a Christian duty. These early hospitals were usually rough buildings with straw on the floor for beds. Patients with all sorts of illnesses were mingled together.

Quarantine 1348 A.D.

Guy de Chauliac, famous surgeon of the Middle Ages, writes concerning the Black Death: "Many were in doubt about the cause of the great mortality. In some places they thought the Jews poisoned the world: and so killed them. In others it was the poor deformed people who were held responsible: and they drove them out. Finally they kept guards in the cities and villages, permitting the entry of no one who was not well known . . ." This is the first use of quarantine. That was in 1348. In 1383 travelers in ships suspected of infection were held for 40 days in the harbor of Marseilles before they were allowed to land. Quarantine means 40. We still use the name, although the time of isolation now varies with the disease.

Surgery 1500

Surgery was long considered inferior to medical practice and was left to barbers, executioners, bath-house keepers and strolling fakers. The physician of the 16th century, dressed in his long robe, disdained to touch the wounded man. With his cane he pointed to the place where the barber should cut. Surgeons staunched the flow of blood with red-hot irons which made a painful wound,

slow to heal. Compassion led the gentle Paré (1536) to use pieces of twine, ligatures, to tie shut the ends of the bleeding vessels. A multitude of ingenious operations, artificial eyes, improved artificial arms and legs, massage, and implanted teeth are some of the things Paré gave to surgery. Nowhere is his character more clearly seen than in his words: "I dressed his wounds; God healed him."

Anatomy 1541

In the second century the Roman physician, Galen, left what purported to be descriptions of the human anatomy, and for fourteen hundred years his word was accepted as authentic. In 1541, Vesalius of Padua discovered that Galen had not dissected human beings, but only beasts. Vesalius determined to describe for the first time true human anatomy. With an artist at his side to draw pictures, he dissected, wrote, described. A year and a half of feverish activity—conducting his dissections on bodies obtained secretly, some from the gallows outside the city—and his great anatomy was ready for the press. It had 663 pages and more than 300 woodcuts. But he had dared to turn against Galen. The scholarly physicians, the teachers of anatomy railed at him. He was ostracized. In indignation he burned his manuscript. When he was dead, men began timidly to look around to see if by chance he was right. They found that he was.

Thermometer 1582

Sanctorius was the first physician to measure body temperature. His thermometer was a long, twisted tube with a bulb nearly as large as an egg at the top; the open end at the bottom was placed in water. The patient held the bulb in his mouth; the air in it, becoming warmed, expanded and escaped through the water. When no more air leaked out, the bulb was taken from the mouth; on cooling, the air contracted and water rose in the tube. The height to which it rose was a measure of the patient's temperature. Sanctorius also counted the pulse. He did not use a watch, for, though watches had been invented in 1510, they still in 1600 had no second, or even minute hand. He used a pendulum and varied the length until the rate of the pendulum corresponded with that of the pulse.

The rate of the pulse was recorded as so many inches of pendulum length.

The Blood 1618

Until the 17th century, every physician had held Galen's view concerning the blood. The liver, so said Galen, was the center of the blood system, where food was mysteriously changed to "natural spirits." He thought of the heart as a churn and a furnace, stirring and heating the blood, while the lungs were fans that cooled it again. William Harvey, English physician of the 17th century, tied a cord about the forearm of a man, tight enough to shut off the flow of the blood in the veins but not in the arteries. With each beat of the heart, blood flowed into the arm, the veins distended, the arm became swollen. Clearly the experiment showed that the blood flowed from the heart through the arteries but did not flow back through them. In 1618, Harvey published his book about the circulation of the blood, and it is one of the great landmarks of medicine.

Microscope 1661

Under the lens of the microscope, invented by Galileo in 1661, the Italian physician, Malpighi, found minute blood vessels connecting the arteries and veins, a thing Harvey could not discern without the lens. But not until the 19th century was it fully known that blood is merely a vehicle, carrying oxygen and good and waste materials from one part of the system to another.

Stethoscope 1819

In auscultation the physician listens to the sounds from the lungs and heart. The gentle "swish" of air as it passes through the tiny bronchial tubes may be altered in disease; the regular "lub-dub" of the normal heartbeat may be blurred with murmurs. Laënnec, in 1819, saw great possibilities in auscultation and also found great difficulties in it. Some patients were so fat that the faint sounds from the chest were lost. He had a fat patient suffering from heart trouble, and not a sound could he get. One day, watching children play on a pile of lumber, he saw one child put his ear to the end of a long beam; another went to the opposite end and tapped on the wood. The signal traveled through the beam. There Laënnec saw an answer to his problem. He hastened to the hospital, took a paper-covered book, rolled it into a cylinder and to the amazement of the onlookers put one end of the crude instrument against the patient's chest and applied his ear to the other. To his joy he heard the heart sounds clearly. Soon he was making little wooden "trumpets" on a turning lathe, and the stethoscope was on its way toward its modern form.

Anesthetics 1842

William T. Morton, a dentist, had experimented with ether on himself, on the family dog, and had used it with success during the extraction of a tooth. He asked Dr. Warren of the Massachusetts General Hospital for permission to administer ether during a major operation. The request was granted. At the appointed time, when the surgeon, the patient, the strong men to hold him down in his struggles and the incredulous spectators were all ready, Morton administered the ether. In a few minutes the patient slept. With the completion of the operation, Dr. Warren turned to the spectators. "Gentlemen, this is no humbug," he said.

Antiseptics 1860

Joseph Lister, a young surgeon in Glasgow in 1860, turned his attention to infection in wounds. He operated skillfully, cared for his patients, yet half or more of them died from blood poisoning. Reading of Pasteur's discovery that wines spoiled due to the growth of bacteria, he saw a similarity between putrefaction of wine and the infection of wounds. So he washed his instruments in carbolic acid; he dipped his hands in it, he sprayed a mist of it into the room. He found that clean wounds heal quickly. Surgical cleanliness, or asepsis, became the dominant idea of surgery.

X ray 1895

The X ray was discovered in 1895 by the physicist, Roentgen. Working in his darkened laboratory he chanced to cover his Crookes tube with black paper to exclude light, then he turned on the electrical discharge. No visible light appeared, but the coated paper glowed with a ghostly light. He picked up the paper and turned its coated surface away from the tube. It continued to glow. He held his hand before it and saw what no one had ever seen before—the shadow of the bones of his hand. The invisible rays were found to affect photographic film. It was possible to take pictures of bone and structures beneath the surface of the skin. Inaccurate news of the discovery leaked out. It was believed that it could be used anywhere, anytime. An English merchant promptly advertised X ray proof clothes for modest ladies. A bill was introduced into the legislature of New Jersey prohibiting the use of X rays in opera glasses. Within a month, however, the X ray was seized upon by physicians and used in medicine, and in the many decades since Roentgen, it has become a most valuable method of diagnosis.

HOWARD W. HAGGARD, M.D.

SCULLY'S THEORY

Frank Scully, that illustrious invalid who brought more laughs to other invalids than anyone I know, had a theory that there was a relationship between illness, assorted physical handicaps and creative talent. As evidence, he would cite the number of poets, writers, composers, philosophers, saints and scientists who suffered from tuberculosis including Edgar Allan Poe, Elizabeth Barrett Browning, John Keats, Walt Whitman, Goethe, Robert Louis Stevenson, Emily Dickinson, Anton Chekhov, Franz Kafka, Ralph Waldo Emerson, Katherine Mansfield, Schiller, Mozart, Chopin, Spinoza, D. H. Lawrence, Henry David Thoreau, Ring Lardner, Eugene O'Neill and Dr. R. T. H. Laënnec, who invented the stethoscope. George Jean Nathan seems to have come to a similar conclusion. He said, "Art is the child of ill health. In the whole history of art there is a negligible record of a completely sound man having produced a notable piece of work."

Frank believed that since certain men of genius worked best when intoxicated, a similar toxic stimulus might account for genius among lungers. In other words, creative achievement is the result of poison. Too much poison, a dead genius. Just enough, a masterpiece. Too little, parsnips. Frank pointed to John Keats as an example of the first and Harold Bell Wright as an example of the last.

If it had not been for his stutter, Somerset Maugham might never have written, *Of Human Bondage,* which is about a man handicapped with a clubfoot. In fact, Frank argued, he might never have become a writer at all. The difficulty of expressing ideas smoothly via the medium of speech can lead to writing them down on paper. This was true not only of Maugham but also of Arnold Bennett and Charles Lamb, both of whom were stammerers.

George Bernard Shaw was poisoned into action by smallpox and an infected foot. Result: *The Doctor's Dilemma.*

Some may argue that plenty of talented people have accomplished great things without having had to call in the doctor first. There is, however, more than one way of developing a toxemia. Bending the elbow—à la Brendan Behan or Dylan Thomas—is certainly one of the most familiar.

Helen Keller was both deaf and blind, but this did not prevent her from becoming outstanding. Others plagued by poor eyesight were John Milton, Theodore Roosevelt, Joseph Pulitzer, Booth Tarkington and Tommy Armour.

The effort and self-discipline a person expends to compete with normal, healthy people gives him so much momentum that sometimes he sails right past them in his endeavors. There are handicaps that some might turn into an advantage, like loss of hearing for Thomas Edison, who might well have needed the peace and quiet for his work on his inventions. Others who might have come to enjoy not hearing minor disturbances were Sam Pepys and the famous painter Sir Joshua Reynolds.

For musicians it could be disastrous to lose their hearing, but Ludwig van Beethoven and Edvard Grieg didn't give up because of that.

Van Gogh obviously subscribed to Frank's theory before Frank even proposed it, and lopped off an ear so as to up the odds in his race for immortality.

Leg amputations rarely kept a good actor or actress down. Sarah Bernhardt, one of the greatest actresses of France, was an amputee. Herbert Marshall, star of stage and screen, had an artificial limb. Although they flourished in an era when journalists were referred to as leg-men, St. John Ervine, Laurence Stallings, Walter Duranty and Frank Scully seemed to function very well on either artificial legs or crutches. Franklin Delano Roosevelt rose to the most powerful position in America when he could not walk one step on his own, the result of his bout with polio. Lord Byron was born with malformations of both feet. At the end of his life, the great painter Auguste Renoir had to have the brush strapped to his arthritic hand.

Michelangelo was severely stricken with intestinal disorders and Frank Harris had to have his stomach pumped almost every day as a result of having had to eat grasshoppers and other indigestible food while traveling in Africa. Others with stomach trouble were Mark Twain, Napoleon, Shakespeare and Nietzsche, not to mention Anthony Trollope, who suffered from gallstones.

A combination of ills and being deprived of faculties often makes people bitter. Frank, however, insisted that an invalid was simply one who allowed "his mind to be put in a splint." People would come to him with their complaints—he called himself "grief commissioner without portfolio"—and would leave counting their blessings.

The story goes that once when a doctor informed him, "Sorry Frank, but I'm going to cut out your appendix," Frank replied, "Go ahead, Doc. I'd rather you do it than my editor."

ALICE SCULLY

"Nurse, Mrs. Brown's case history . . . Volume 4."

Cartoon by DAVID HARBAUGH, © 1966 by *Modern Medicine.*

*"Has it ever occurred to you that we're
the somebodies nobody's worse off than?"*

Cartoon by J. FARRIS, © 1964 by Saturday Review, Inc.

ACT **V** *Horizontal Blues*

The days when you're feeling particularly sorry for yourself seem to be the days people keep telling you to "Cheer up!"

But why should you?

What is there to bang the bedpan about?

Haven't you been lashed to the sheets since the end of the Ice Age?

Haven't the dead petals of the doctor's rosy promises fluttered out of the window long ago?

Don't you feel that your friends are acting restive because you must rest in béd so long?

As if to say, "Isn't it about time you got up and stopped squeezing us dry of sympathy?"

Do they expect *you* to play Pollyanna and cheer *them* up?

Haven't you got troubles enough without that?

On those days when the future seems so far away (and not a present in sight) there's nothing to do but shift your mind out of low.

If you can't sleep the blues off, just turn over to a new leaf and let's get on with the show.

DOWN AND OUT FOR THE COUNT

Dr. Jones, a young physician with a growing practice, had been going night and day for the better part of a week. If it wasn't the stork busy in one part of the town it was the malaria microbe busy in another. He kept up his round of visits until exhausted nature demanded a respite.

He staggered into his house in the evening completely fagged out and tumbled into bed, telling his wife that, excepting upon a matter of life and death, he was not to be called.

At two o'clock in the morning she came to his bedside, shook him, pinched him, slapped him in the face with a wet washrag and finally roused him to a state of semi-consciousness. Mrs. Smith, physically the biggest woman in town, had been seized with a heart attack at her home on the next street and he was wanted immediately.

He struggled to his feet, threw a few garments on over his nightclothes, caught up his emergency kit and in a sort of walking trance made his way to the Smith residence. A frightened member of the household led him to the sick-room. There the patient lay, a great mountain of flesh, her features congested and her breath coming in laborious panting. Dr. Jones took her pulse and her temperature and examined her eyes, her lips and her tongue. Then he perched himself in a half recumbent attitude upon the side of the bed, put his right ear against her left breast and said, "Madam, will you kindly start counting very slowly? Now then, one-two-three and so on. Go on until I tell you to stop."

Obediently the sufferer began.

The next thing Dr. Jones knew was when a shaft of bright morning sunlight fell upon his face, and, drowsily, he heard a faint, weak female voice saying, "Nine thousand seven hundred and one, nine thousand seven hundred and two . . ."

IRVIN S. COBB

BUSY SIGNALS

When department-store executive David May was a patient in a Los Angeles hospital, he was told that one friend—and one only—might phone him there. May chose Frank Clark, but then told other friends to use that name in calling. One "Frank Clark" who called was told by the operator, "Sorry, Mr. Clark, but he's talking to you right now—and also you're on the other line waiting to speak to him next."

LEONARD LYONS

WOULD YOU BELIEVE

One surgeon in every thousand is lefthanded. *No statistics are available as to how many are underhanded.*

Chinese used to pay their doctors only while they were well. *In other countries doctor bills make people sick.*

Babies are supposed to be able to hear four months before birth, *so watch what you say to expectant mothers.*

Male babies are more likely to be the result of conception between July and September (April–July babies). *This is what's known as a summer son.*

In 1934 there were 16,000 "Visiting Nurses" in America. *By 1967 there are 16,000 less; the visitors went home.*

In the old West blacksmiths were called in to knock out teeth with a chisel and sledgehammer. *Now I know where my dentist learned his trade.*

Harold Rickett, of Sandusky, Michigan, when twelve years old, was found to have two appendixes—*so the doctor charged him double.*

Surgery was originally the function of barbers and executioners and was a despised trade up till the nineteenth century. *Let's go back to those good old days.*

Back in the Depression days, a doctor in a factory town, Dr. G. A. Smale mailed out bills marked "Paid in full" for Christmas to patients who needed it. Felt it would make them better faster. *The A.M.A. has never forgiven him.*

One London doctor invented a foot-long brush to scrub tonsils. Claimed cleaning and disinfecting them by brushing twice a day would eliminate necessity of removal by surgery. *Of course he got a lot of business removing the brushes.*

Doctors have had such differences of opinion at times, when called in consultation, that Dr. Laszlo Farkas and Dr. Joseph Krauss, old friends in Budapest, Hungary, felt so intensely they finally dueled over whether an operation would be helpful or not. This as late as August 1935. *The only thing American doctors split over is fees.*

Kolesnikof, a cobbler in Russia, masqueraded as a doctor, became chief surgeon of the Kiev hospitals, and performed 600 major surgeries with great success before he was exposed. Success was attributed to the speed with which he operated, thereby avoiding hemorrhages and shock. *Where's the nearest shoe repair stand?*

BOB LANE

When an old roué resident of our town collapsed, he was taken to a hospital, where, semiconscious, he heard the doctor point out to the two student nurses with him that now was the time for them to learn mouth-to-mouth resuscitation. At this, the patient raised a shaky finger and pointed to one of the nurses—a cute little blonde. "Teach her first!" he whispered.

WILLIAM J. KIEWEL

What are the most delicious scents? Everyone could make a list. Mine would contain sweetbrier in the air, so vague and elusive that search cannot trace the source. Pine trees on a hot day. Mint sauce. Newly split wood. Cinnamon. Ripe apples. Tea just opened. Coffee just ground. A racing stable. A dairy farm. Cigars in a box. A circus. And I have said nothing of flowers!

E. V. LUCAS

LIPSTICK SIGN

One of the best indicators of progress and recovery in a sick female patient, according to Dr. Mario N. Fabi, writing in *Pennsylvania Medicine,* is the lipstick sign.

"When a woman is ill," Dr. Fabi declares, "she usually stops applying makeup. As recovery ensues, there comes a time when she again dons lipstick. This is the lipstick sign. It is as if the patient had some deep inner awareness of the initiation of the recovery process, even before the physician is able to recognize it. . . ."

Well water is water that won't make you sick.

Heretics is what you get from your father and mother.

It is important to take careful care of our bodies, for where would we be without them?

"I don't mind them sneaking in an occasional piece of pie, but . . ."

Cartoon by SLIM, © 1966 by *Modern Medicine.*

The humorous vein supplies blood to the funny bone.

A scarlet is a little scar.

Men can reach maturity but only women have reached maternity so far.

Everybody has a thyroid gland which helps the body burn up food so why do we cook it in the first place?

Appendixes are useless things that everybody still has left over from some surplus body.

Nowadays everything is specialized. The brain specializes in thinking and the muscles specialize in working. It used to be different somehow.

Trunks are for storing valuables in, so the human trunk contains such valuables as stomachs, hearts and a lot of other stuff.

The sternum is the bone we sit on.

The patella is the knee. Water on the knee is called flotilla.

The iris is the pleasant part of the eye, like in iris eyes are smiling.

Sounds are vibrations of our vice box.

There are cavities all through our bodies. That is all right as long as they don't get into our teeth.

Everybody is either a man or a woman. Nobody is neutral.

Veins could very well be called something else if it were not for the lack of a better name.

Metabolism is a way of changing matter into energy without having to mess around with atoms.

Without red cells, blood would bleed to death.

The way to remember a body cell from a prison cell is that they are in people instead of people in them.

To waist away means to go on a diet.

In our study of anatomy last year I was Chairman of the Hind Bone Section.

A mutation is a change of body while a transmutation is a change of trains.

The three races of man are The Kentucky Derby, Belmont and The Preakness.

The biceps and triceps are in the arm, but forceps are usually found in the mouth.

The body has more cells in adulthood than in any of the other hoods.

Skin is used to hold people in. It is the original corsit.

To upbraid somebody means to fix their hair.

When you breathe in you inhale and when you breathe out you expectorate.

Harvested by ART LINKLETTER

Bob Hope tells of the English doctor, looking over the charts in a London hospital, who was interested in the system of abbreviations: S.F. for Scarlet Fever; T.B. for Tuberculosis.

All the charts seemed to indicate a favorable progress except one that was labeled G.O.K.

The doctor called one of the staff physicians. "Just what is G.O.K.?"

"Oh that? It means we can't diagnose it. God Only Knows."

FRANCIS LEO GOLDEN

Nellie Nifty, R.N.

"The nurses on TV always have time
for long heart-to-heart talks."

Cartoon by KAZ, © 1966 by *Modern Medicine.*

"Mrs. Smithe felt ill. She went home."

Cartoon by KAZ, © 1964 by *Modern Medicine.*

"If she bets you a penny you can't
touch your toes, don't fall for it."

Cartoon by KAZ, © 1966 by *Modern Medicine.*

"He's tried everything—rum,
scotch, whiskey, vodka . . ."

Cartoon by KAZ, © 1966 by *Modern Medicine.*

The shots I get of penicillin
are not put in the spot I'm ill in.

ANNA HERBERT

Jean Louis Forain, French artist, was on his death-bed and his relatives were trying to simulate confidence in his recovery. "You're looking much better," his wife assured him. "The color has come back into your cheeks," said his son. "You're breathing easier, Father," his daughter observed.

Forain smiled weakly. "Thank you," he whispered. "I'm going to die cured."

BENNETT CERF

An essayist at the New York State Medical Society Convention in Albany remarked that physicians every day are called on to accept cases that are personally distasteful. "But Somerset Maugham, who is a brother M.D., once pointed out that men, for their soul's good, should each day do two things they disliked."

A colleague in the audience addressed the essayist. "Did Maugham practice what he preached?"

"Yes," replied the essayist. "I once heard him say that he followed this precept scrupulously. Every morning he got out of bed and every night he got into bed."

FRANCIS LEO GOLDEN

LIMERICK

No matter how grouchy you're feeling,
You'll find the smile more or less healing.
　　It grows in a wreath
　　All around the front teeth—
Thus preserving the face from congealing.

JOHN ARMSTRONG

THE SQUEEZED LEMON TREES

Frank Scully was once asked to give the main address at a dinner at a convention of the National Society for Crippled Children and Adults in Chicago. This is what he said:

Two days before I left Hollywood to come to Chicago, I was interviewed by Gloria Swanson on her radio program. Preceding me was Marjorie Lawrence, the Australian opera star who now does her singing from a wheelchair. I met Miss Lawrence with the warmth and delight of a buck private who had got out of an awful bad bombing. She acted as delighted to see me as I was to see her. Every time I meet someone who had been through a mill similar to my own, I feel that same way.

You see, I have been a veteran of so many hospitals that when I meet a person who has also come through, I first am not only happy, but second, I want to know how they did it. They frequently are inarticulate in the matter. They don't know how they did it, they groped their way through. I am a little bit more clear as to how and why I did it.

First, I had wonderful friends; second, I had something which is superior to a sense of humor. I had a sense of proportion and I didn't think that it was so serious whether I lived or died. But since I was apparently going to live, I was determined that I had to give back to God and all His lovely children as much of what I could in the years that were left to me.

Since I figured life as so much velvet and should have been dead years before, I didn't have the peculiar kind of fear that most other people had. I had fears, but not the standard sort, and so I was credited and regarded in many places as a guy of terrific courage. It wasn't terrific, it was just different. Of course, like others, I wanted to make the best of myself and stand up and walk.

I think that today employers and others accept the fact that you are not a cripple just because parts of your body don't work like other people's bodies. In fact, my solace is that you are not crippled at all unless your mind is in a splint. I only feel sorry for people who have physical infirmities and a mind that doesn't give them a chance. After all, the body is of this earth, but the spirit is for eternity, and the mind is the great thing and the greatest loss. Thus we who are suffering in one small way should have the greatest compassion and the greatest prayers for those who are really mentally ill.

I want to tell you about a parable of the squeezed lemon tree. This is the real theme of my talk. I had two dwarf lemon trees that grew about two feet high and were kept in vases at the entrance to Bedside Manor, my home in Hollywood. One day they began to die. I called in a tree surgeon who looked the trees over and said that they were dwarfs and had become rooted. His advice was to throw them away.

Well, I'm different from most people. When I get advice like that I throw the expert away. So, I took the crippled little things and transplanted them to a lower slope of the garden where they could get more sun. I watered them well and watched them, and during the year they began to come to life—in two years they began to grow. In three years they reached twenty feet in the air, although previously they had been living for eight years as dwarfs. They blossomed, they began to bear fruit, and now they produce so much fruit that we can't keep ourselves out of the way of lemons.

The moral, it seems to me, is that if we can do that for crippled, squeezed lemon trees, why can't we do as well for crippled, squeezed people?

"That was the doctor with his diagnosis, dear! . . .
He says if you feel better tomorrow,
you had the 24-hour virus."

ACT VI *Exit Smiling*

Your doctor, who seemed to have lost all interest in you, *you, the most interesting case he ever had*, suddenly likes the look of your chart and orders you to go home.

Before you know it he has ordered the nurses to let you walk around, and he is writing "Discharged" on your chart and signing your release.

Oh, happy days! To shake hands with all those who have helped you on your way, to wish those still in bed your own break in luck, to walk out of your linen prison into the sunlight and finally to eat at last that particular meal you've been wanting ever since you got into the place—oh, happy daze!

You've left a dozen things undone. You forgot to tip the orderly, say goodbye to the night nurse, or get the address of that patient you liked down the hall.

Well, the mail is still operating and you may recall how often *you* prayed for letters when you were in the hospital. Write them. Thank them, pan them, praise them, but *write* them.

Here are a couple of laughs and a final thought for the road.

The soldier was being given a blood test. The inexperienced young nurse jabbed him twenty times before she contacted a vein.

The soldier hung around. "What are you waiting for?" asked the nurse. The soldier looked at her shyly. "My Purple Heart, miss."

FRANCIS LEO GOLDEN

Cartoon by Bob Zahn, © 1965 by *Modern Medicine*.

"My, what a lovely bunch of get-well cards—all from the hospital nursing staff."

Cartoon by LARRY HARRIS, © 1964 by *Modern Medicine*.

"In layman's terms, your stomach and liver seem to have formed a suicide pact."

Cartoon by BOB BARNES, © 1966 by The Register and Tribune Syndicate, Inc.

DEFINITIONS FROM WEBSTER'S UNAFRAID DICTIONARY

Allergy. Something a doctor says you have when he does know what it is—but doesn't know how to get rid of it.—AL BERNIE

Anesthesia. An aroma coma.

Antidote. A medicine you take to prevent dotes. —Overheard by ART LINKLETTER

Baby. A sample of humanity entirely surrounded by yell; a person who eats twice as much as he weighs every year.

Backache. Man's greatest labor saving device. —JOE RYAN

Bacteria. The only culture many children are exposed to.—BERT KRUSE

Birth. The first and direst of all disasters.—AMBROSE BIERCE

Body. The chief function of the body is to carry the brain around.—THOMAS A. EDISON

Breathing. A form of life insurance.

Cough. A convulsion of the lungs, vellicated by some sharp serosity. It is pronounced *coff*.—DR. SAM'L JOHNSON

Diabetes. The malfunction of the organ that makes sugar a bitter pill.

Diapers. The humble banners of fertility.—BRUCE HUTCHINSON

Diet. No matter what kind you are on, you can usually eat as much as you want of anything you don't like.—WALTER SLEZAK

Dieting. Breaking the pound barrier.—RICHARD WHALLEY

Drugs, wonder. We're so well supplied with many kinds
In bottle, tube and jar:
They've been so long upon the shelf
We wonder what they are!
—S. OMAR BARKER

Drugstore. A telephone booth with lunch counter attached.

Druggist. A man who is paid for counting pills.

Electrocardiograph. Ticker tape.—LIL O. OLSEN

Euphoria. Feeling so good, you are over the weather.

Father. A thing that is forced to endure child-birth without an anesthetic.—PAUL HARVEY

Gargle. Hoarse liniment.—EDWARD NIETUPSKI

Germs. Sort of small insecks that swim in you when they can get in. Some are called measles, but you can't see them.—ANON., JR. (*British Division*)

Hiccoughs. Messages from departed spirits.

Hospital. A pain factory.—FRANK SCULLY

Immune. To do it with a needle.—ANON., JR.

Immunity. The ability to catch a disease without the aid of a physician.—ANON., JR.

Insomnia. What a person has when he lies awake all night for an hour.—ROGER PRICE

Life. A disease from which sleep gives us relief every sixteen hours.—CHAMFORT

A grindstone. Whether it grinds you down or polishes you up depends on what you're made of. —ANON.

Lunacy. A condition where dreams overflow into life.—CONNOLLY NORMAN

Lungs. Those wonderful windbags.—J. D. RATCLIFF

Madman. One who suffers from absence of mind.

Man. The animal who gets pleasure from doing those things which give him no pleasure.—LATAPIL

Maternity Ward. The only place in the world where there isn't a chance of evading the issue. —SUPERIOR CIRKUTS

Medicine. We've made great medical progress in the last generation. What used to be merely an itch is now an allergy.—SUNSHINE MAGAZINE

Medical specialization has reached such a state today that patients have to learn to diagnose themselves before they know which specialist to call.—TWO MINUTES WITH YOU

Medicine, socialized. Giving free diagnoses at parties.—ANON.

Mother. A kid's bosom friend. **Smart mother.** One who knows a pounce of prevention is worth a pound of cure.—IMOGENE FEY

Nurse, registered. A dame who shakes you at 2 A.M. and says, "Wake up—it's time to take your sleeping pill."

Patient. A large body of pain surrounded by cures.—FRANK SCULLY

Penicillin. A medicine which, if you are full of and sneeze, you can cure somebody.

Pharmacy. A department store with a prescription counter.—CHANGING TIMES

Philosopher. A person who knows how to take anything that doesn't happen to him.

Physician. A doctor who treats what you have. **Specialist.** A doctor who thinks you have what he treats.—CHANGING TIMES

Sixty: When it takes longer to rest than to get tired.

Specialist. A doctor consulted at the last minute to share the blame.—ANON.

Stethoscope. A magnifying glass for looking into people's chest with the ears.—ANON., JR.

Whiskey. By far the most popular of all the many remedies that absolutely won't cure a cold. —Quoted by EARL WILSON

Gathered by LEONARD L. LEVINSON

Dr. W. F. McDonald describes his soft, tiptoeing walk through the pediatric ward well after midnight, lest he awaken any of his little patients. Near the last bed he noticed an opened box of chocolates and helped himself to one.

Next day during visiting hours he was in the ward again. A child at the far corner spotted him. The youngster's voice rang through the room. All eyes immediately centered on the doctor. "There he is, Mom," shrilled the boy, "there's the doctor who swiped my candy."

FRANCIS LEO GOLDEN

All the sleep I need is another five minutes.

WILSON MIZNER

FANTASY WITHOUT DRUGS

It is 1984. The scene is the New York apartment of Dr. Arthur Jones and his wife, Emmy. It is an autumn evening; the doctor has just come in from a hard day at the office.

EMMY: I have a splitting headache. Is there an aspirin left in the house?

ARTHUR (*looking around furtively*):   Of course not. You know that the last bottle of aspirin was smuggled in from Europe when we came back from our trip a year ago, and the last tablet went a while back.

EMMY: Well, what am I going to do?

ARTHUR: Have you tried the dandelion tea? I picked a bagful in the park only a few months ago.

EMMY: That was used up when Jimmy had pneumonia. I've also tried the heating pad and a mustard plaster and they didn't do a bit of good.

ARTHUR (*pouring the drinks*):   Well, take a double Scotch. It's a lucky thing that whiskey and cigarettes didn't come under the Drug Abolition Act.

EMMY: What I don't understand is how you can practice medicine without medicine. Don't you get discouraged sometimes?

ARTHUR: Why, no, not really. You just do the best you can. Back in seventy-six when the Senate Subcommittee found out that the few drugs still left were causing side effects they recommended abolishing all drugs. The Christian Scientists put on a publicity campaign using the slogan "The Fifth Freedom: Freedom from Drugs," you remember. The doctors, the pharmacists and the drug firms all fought it, but they were accused of trying to make money while people suffered drug reactions. None of us wanted to stick our necks out and be charged with hurting our patients; so we didn't fight hard enough, I suppose. The anti-cancer, the anti-hypertensive and the anti-depressant compounds had all been withdrawn in the late sixties as being too dangerous. So, on July Fourth, 1976, every prescription drug and patent medicine was made illegal for commerce, putting an end to drug reactions once and for all.

EMMY: But what can you do for your patients now?

ARTHUR: Oh, we still can do surgery, although a new Senate Committee is looking into surgical complications at the moment and anything can happen. Besides, it's hard to do without anesthetics. Psychoanalysis has been labeled a "dangerous procedure for investigational use only" because it isn't absolutely safe. We are still permitted to do acupunctures and cuppings. I just heard of something encouraging today: Someone is developing a new system of medicine. You make an effigy of the patient and treat it. In that way, nobody gets hurt.

EMMY: But nobody ever gets helped either. Look what happened to Jimmy (*sniffles*).

ARTHUR: There, now. Have another drink.

EMMY: I only wish we had flown Jimmy to Mexico on the Mercy Service that the Mexican Government set up last year so that he could have had some antibiotics.

ARTHUR: Well, things aren't completely hopeless here. We still can prescribe placebos.

EMMY: Did you get a chance to read the paper today? There is a piece about placebos (*picking up paper and reading*):"Because of the increasing incidence of adverse affects being reported, the Subcommittee on Dangerous Medical Procedures has recommended that, effective January First, 1985, only half-strength placebos be manufactured."

(*Curtain*)

SIDNEY COHEN, M.D.

A glib-tongued wise guy barged into the office of a Buffalo M.D. one evening and in a voice honeyed with personality asked, "What's the tariff, Doc, to give me a check-up?"

"I'll examine you for ten dollars," answered the doctor.

"O.K., Doc, and if you find it, I'll give you half."

IT COULD BE WORSE

It seems that people who are able
To read a book can't read a label,
Can't comprehend, when feeling aily,
How many times is "three times daily,"
Can't tell if it's a large or wee spoon
When very plainly it says "teaspoon,"
Can't figure out the go-ahead time
When it is written, "Take at bedtime."

The way they phone to ask repeatedly
(Some doctors answer rather heatedly)
To have the label's words translated
And very simple terms equated,
We're only glad that they're not needing
Such help as this with *all* their reading.

RICHARD ARMOUR

HOW TO GET BETTER

*Think of Your Troubles to Come As If
They Were Already Passed and Soon
They Will Be Laughable Memories.*

With one lung, one leg, one kidney, and one idea, a writer like myself can't go on forever, especially if the old pump says no dice. But, if you have most of your vital organs in reasonably good order, there is no reason why anybody can't take the run-of-the-mill maladies and operations in his stride and live to brag about what pushovers they were.

As a general thing I talk very little about the fights microbes have staged using my body as their arena. I know that it's fairly easy to tell people to buck up when their troubles are in the present and yours are in the past. But to show you how I've always thought of mine in the past, let me tell you a story of how superior I can act toward people far better physically than I ever was.

About one year after my leg amputation I was in a Paris restaurant with Walter Duranty. Now, at the time I was a nobody and he was the greatest foreign correspondent in the world. But a nobody or a somebody, on one leg or lying down, there isn't a guy in the world who can push me around in a give-and-take conversation. If I could write the way I can talk I'd make Shakespeare read as badly as Shaw.

So when I sit down to a table I sit down with equals. When I sit down to a typewriter, however, I know I'm behind a whole row of eight balls, and those eight balls are my betters in the field of belles-lettres.

But Duranty and I were sitting down to dinner. We were dining. We were wining. We were half seas over. We were guests of some Syrian tycoon. He was rich but unimportant. I think we both felt superior to him, and I know I felt superior to Duranty.

The reason I did was because I was making Duranty talk about himself. Any reporter feels superior to the person he is interviewing. Sometimes he feels so superior he doesn't pay any attention to what the celebrity is saying and then goes off and writes the wrong story.

So I was feeling superior to Duranty because I was asking him about artificial legs and he was telling me about the best of them and the best were British and because Duranty was British and he thought the best were British and I was feeling superior to him. And then I led with a left and asked him how he lost his leg and he led with his chin and told me how it happened, and then I felt more superior to him than ever.

It seems he was taking a train from Paris to Le Havre and they came upon a wreck. The conductor with French politeness, even under duress, asked him and a companion if they would mind walking beyond the wreck, where another train would take them on to their destination. They crawled over the wreckage to the train beyond and after their baggage was installed, they settled down to the business of continuing their journey.

But the French never do anything by halves, so they sent another train crashing into the one where Duranty and his companion had installed themselves, and Duranty came out of the new wreck with one of his legs bobbed below the knee. Out of this personal catastrophe he got $10,000.

Nellie Nifty, R.N.

*"One good thing—he finally beat
the fifty-dollar-deductible clause."*

Cartoon by KAZ, © 1966 by *Modern Medicine.*

*"Modern techniques are amazing. It's hard to believe
he's only two days out of surgery."*

Cartoon by KAZ, © 1963 by KAZ.

And this changed his life. For a dozen years he had been doing great work for his paper (*The Times*) in Russia and after every ten scoops he asked for a raise. But his paper, being capitalist-minded, thought Duranty, being communist-minded, should be satisfied with the honor of being the best correspondent in Europe.

Never being more than ten steps ahead of bankruptcy Duranty couldn't afford to say, "Outside with that ideology. A raise or I walk!"

But when that $10,000 came to him all in one lump his courage began to climb like a rigged stock. He could, he reasoned, live four years on $10,000 and if his paper didn't give him the raise he was entitled to he was quitting. He cabled them the bad news collect.

Somehow the way the words were arranged this time produced a different effect on the front office. They feared he meant what he said for a change. So they changed their tune too.

Of course, they replied, he could have the raise. Why didn't he ask for it before?

Well, from that time on, with $10,000 in the bank and only one leg to stand on, Duranty became twice as good a reporter as he had been before.

It was always in the back of his head: If they don't like this, I can quit and live for four years without a worry in the world. On that sort of stuff he climbed to the top of the Mt. Everest of Journalism—the Pulitzer Prize for the best reporting of the year.

When he finished telling me his story there was very little left of the champagne and as far as I was concerned even less left of me. But what was still present was all admiration for this leg-man who conquered the world as soon as the ironic gods took one of his legs away.

Still, I couldn't show him what a sucker I had been for his success story. With my right leg amputated only a year before to within six inches of the hip I was a bigger guy than Duranty, who after all had one and three-quarter legs to stand on, I kept telling myself. I had to keep that old superiority complex going.

So instead of saluting him as my hero of the day, which he was, I stopped him with "Duranty, that's the funniest story I've heard in years. You're a howl."

"What do you mean, a howl?" he demanded as if they were fighting words.

"Well," I said, "I've met a lot of screwballs in my time but you're the first one I ever met who was raised on a cut!"

My own gag sent me into such belly-laughter that I practically rolled under the table and brought Duranty with me. We both collapsed from our own laughter, and from that day to this I've never been the same.

I keep living for the day when fate will cuff me just hard enough to leave me reasonably as I am at present and at the same time enrich me by $10,000 so that I can say to editors and publishers, "Nuts to you. Either I get top dough or I walk. I can live four years on this money."

But I'm afraid it will never happen in any such dramatic way. I will have to keep plugging along, nicking my courage out of granite with my fingernails and always living in the future rather than the intolerable present.

You see, I have never been without pain in twenty-seven years, so when I tell you how to get better by thinking of your troubles to come as if they had already passed your door, I'm not telling you something I cribbed from a textbook.

I'm telling you how to conquer pain when all else fails, and in telling you that, I'm confessing that pain is the only thing I'm afraid of. The normal fears of normal people are as remote from me as Ruth amid the alien corn, but pain takes all the guts I have. If, like me, you must endure pain, remember that most of them have a far shorter life than you have. Two or three days is a long run for most pains. The majority run their course in twenty-four hours. So if you can think of today as tomorrow you're telescoping time, and time is the life-blood of pain.

Today's pain cashes in its chips tomorrow. So root for tomorrow and say nuts to today!

FRANK SCULLY

Answers

Answers to Anagrams on Pages 25 to 27.

I

M U S E with R
S E R U M

O A T S with T
T O A S T

R O B E with P
P R O B E

M A N E with E
E N E M A

T H A W with R
W R A T H

R A T E with H
H E A R T

R U N S with E
N U R S E

T H E E with R
E T H E R

II

VOTER
ASIDE
CROWD
ROUGE
DEVOUR

RAVEN
SHAME
TABLE
ALOUD
BRACE

III

TROWEL
GARDEN
DIVANS
AIGRET
ADMIRE

ASLANT
APPEAL
SPINET
DINERS
TOCSIN

IV

RACED
SACRED
CREASED
TABLE
BLEATS
BLASTED

DANGER
ANGERED
DERANGED
STAPLE
PLASTER
REPLATES

V

WARBLE
GARBLE
RABBLE
BAILER

BLAMED
GAMBLE
BEDLAM
MARBLE

VI

WITHDRAW
TOPMOST
NATURAL
CURTAIN
KNAVISH

REVERSES
INTRIGUE
RELATING
GLUCOSE
RECHARGED

VII

AMUSE
MEANS
MARES
REAMS
LAMES
MALES

SEAMS
SMEAR
BEAMS
DAMES
GAMES
TAMES

Answer to Sun, Moon and Planets Puzzle on Page 28.

1. Sun
2. Mercury
3. Venus
4. Earth
5. Moon
6. Mars
7. Jupiter
8. Saturn
9. Uranus
10. Neptune
11. Pluto

Answer to Armchair Tour of the U.S.A. Puzzle on Page 29.

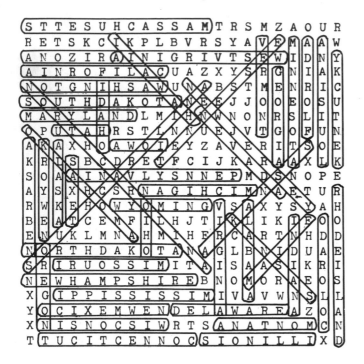

Answer to Months of the Year Puzzle on Page 30.

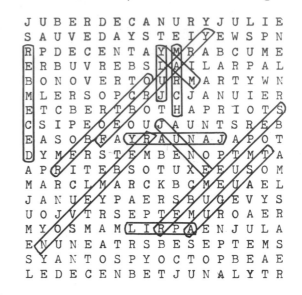

Answer to Days of the Week Puzzle on Page 30.

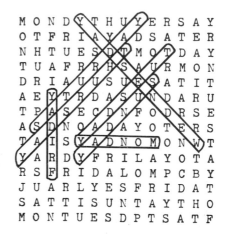

Answer to Line-drawing Puzzle on Page 31.

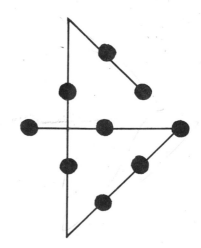

Suggested Answers to Color Quiz on Page 31.

Red	*Redbook* (magazine)
Blue	Blue jay (bird)
Green	*Green Mansions* (book)
White	"White Christmas" (song)
Black	Black lily (flower) *Black Narcissus* (book)
Yellow	Yellowtail (fish), Canary (bird)
Pink	Hyacinth (flower)
Purple	Pansy (flower)
Gray	Gray's "Elegy"
Orange	Poppy (flower)

Answers to Quiz on Pages 31–32.

Sentence Completions:

1. If your garden plot is small, it will not pay to grow crops which require a large amount of space in order to develop.

2. The American colonies were separate and distinct entities, each having its own government and being entirely independent.

3. Iron rusts from disuse, stagnant water loses its purity; even so does inaction sap the vigor of the mind.

4. Since growth is not a uniform process for all people, the importance of studying the individual growth pattern has been emphasized.

5. If we cannot make the wind blow when and where we wish it to blow, we can at least make use of its force.

Analogies:

1. Borderland:Country—(C) Margin:Page
2. Tree:Forest—(D) Voice:Chorus
3. Grove:Tree—(E) Archipelago:Island
4. Lamps:Darkness—(A) Books:Ignorance
5. Ointment:Burn—(B) Sympathy:Sorrow
6. Calamity:Distress—(B) Triumph:Exultation
7. Trigger:Bullet—(D) Switch:Current

How well did *you* reason?

Answers to Your Literary I.Q. Quiz on Page 32.

1. BEACON
2. ECONOMIST
3. FALCON
4. ICONOCLAST
5. DEACON
6. GASCON
7. MISCONSTRUE
8. CONDEMN
9. NONCONFORMIST
10. ABSCOND
11. UNCONSCIOUS
12. ZIRCON
13. OVERCONFIDENT
14. RECONNOITER
15. RACONTEUR

Answers to "Name Ten of Each" on Page 33.

1. *Composer:* Ludwig van Beethoven, Johann Sebastian Bach, Johannes Brahms, Wolfgang Mozart, Edvard Grieg, Richard Wagner, Jean Sibelius, Ignace Paderewski, Leopold Godowski, Johann Strauss

2. *Kinds of fur:* Mink, Beaver, Sable, Rabbit, Otter, Caracul, Squirrel, Seal, Chincilla, Fox

3. *Fish:* Cod, Mackerel, Pike, Bass, Sardines, Flounder, Tuna, Halibut, Salmon, Haddock

4. *Writers:* William Shakespeare, Ernest Hemingway, George Bernard Shaw, Frank Scully, Carl Sandburg, Jean Baptiste Molière, James Baldwin, Will Durant, Upton Sinclair, Willa Cather

5. *Bodies of water:* Atlantic, Caribbean, Baltic, Gulf of Mexico, Sea of Japan, Mediterranean, Pacific, North Sea, Adriatic, Arctic

6. *Flowers:* Rose, Forget-me-not, Tulip, Pansy, Marigold, Petunia, Daffodil, Bluebell, Daisy, Buttercup

7. *Articles of clothing:* Shoes, Cloak, Vest, Pants, Shirt, Dress, Slip, Pajamas, Coat, Sweater

8. *Best friends:* Your individual choice.

9. *Operas:* Aïda, Carmen, Tosca, Faust, Lohengrin, La Bohême, Cavalleria Rusticana, William Tell, La Traviata, Pagliacci

10. *Books:* The Bible, The *Odyssey, Don Quixote, Gone with the Wind, Crime and Punishment, The Story of Philosophy, Lord Jim, So Big, Grapes of Wrath, A Treasury of the World's Great Letters*

11. *Food for breakfast:* Bacon and eggs, Toast, Orange juice, cereal, English muffins, Hot cakes, Hashed brown potatoes, Sweet roll, Coffee, Milk

12. *Food for lunch:* Sandwich, Chocolate malt, Hamburger, Coke, Éclair, Salad, Omelet, Tortillas, Pizza, Hash

13. *Food for dinner:* Soup, Corned beef and cabbage, Steak, Roast beef, Chicken cacciatore, Spaghetti, Lasagna, Lobster Newburg, Bouillabaisse, Chow mein

14. *Titles of poems:* "To a Skylark," "Ode on a Grecian Urn," "A Few Figs from Thistles," "Childe Harold," "Midnight Ride of Paul Revere," "Tamerlane," "Hiawatha," "The Charge of the Light Brigade," "Il Penseroso," "Leaves of Grass"

15. *Counties in your own state:* Depends on where you live.

16. *Favorite actors:* Individual choice.

17. *Favorite movies:* Individual choice.

18. *Trees:* Birch, Elm, Oak, Maple, Fir, Pine, Sequoia, Ash, Hickory, Mahogany

19. *Adages:* He who hesitates is lost. Look before you leap. Better late than never. The early bird catches the worm. A stitch in time saves nine. Never judge a book by its cover. Birds of a feather flock together. Familiarity breeds contempt. Absence makes the heart grow fonder. There is always someone worse off than yourself.

20. *Rivers:* Mississippi, Volga, Danube, Thames, Rhine, Seine, Tigris, Hudson, Tiber, Jordan

Answers to Hidden Words on Page 33.

Flower	M E T A N I P R Z U K I	Petunia
Bird	B R E A L U G K E M	Eagle
Color	K N R B E R R U L	Blue
Vegetable	H U A D E S M I D Z R	Radish
Tree	S L U D E X M A P	Elm
Fruit	A Z O M R T P S U L	Plum
Girl's name	V P L N I T A Z Y S	Sylvia
Boy's name	S L E R U T O K E B R	Robert

Suggested Answers on Things Not Found on a Desert Island, Page 33.

1. Toothbrush	11. Bookmark
2. Pen	12. Nail file
3. Comb	13. Screwdriver
4. Broom	14. Hammer
5. Towel	15. Step stool
6. Chair	16. Money
7. Telephone	17. Scissors
8. Stamp	18. Handbag
9. Cup	19. Car
10. Pot holder	20. Kleenex

Answer to "Information Desk" Crossword on Page 34.

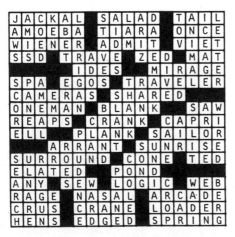

Answer to "Change of Face" Crossword on Page 35.

Answer to "Getting the Picture" Crossword on Page 36.

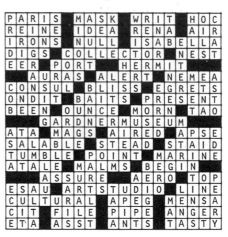

Answers to Utopias on Page 37.

Dark to Dawn	Low to Top	Wan to Fun
darn	tow	fan
dawn	top	fun

Vale to Hill	Boy to Man	Awake to Smoke
hale	bay	awoke
hall	may	amoke
hill	man	smoke

Wet to Dry	Sick to Jake	Cat to Dog
bet	sack	rat
bat	lack	rag
bay	lace	lag
day	lake	log
dry	Jake	dog

Coma to Talk	*Dolt to Sage*	*Hurt to Well*	*Fear to None*	*Temp to Norm*	*Broken to Mended*
come	dole	hurl	rear	tamp	broker
came	dope	hull	real	tame	booker
tame	rope	hell	reel	time	booked
tale	rape	heal	reed	lime	looked
talk	rage	weal	rend	line	locked
	sage	well	mend	lint	lacked
			mind	link	backed
Drain to Dried	*Walk to Jump*	*Near to Fame*	mine	lank	banked
train	wack	neat	dine	land	banker
trait	sack	meat	done	lard	bander
trail	suck	meet	none	lord	bender
trall	sunk	melt		nord	mender
trill	suns	malt		norm	mended
trial	runs	male			
triad	rums	sale			
driad	rump	same			
dried	jump	fame			